Here's what others are saying about, **"Growing Up Whitney."**

"He made me read it."
    - Brad Barrett

"I just couldn't put it down. He wouldn't let me."
    - Pat Sokoll

"I felt I had to look at it."
    - John Meyer

"Is he still talking about Fathering?"
    - Brent Knox

*"Neva told me that if I didn't read it,
Rick would probably cry."*
    – Chris Biang

Growing Up Whitney

Raising Kids to Stand in the Gap

by Rick Whitney

a Great Commission Northwest book

Growing Up Whitney
Raising Kids to Stand in the Gap

Published by *Great Commission Northwest*.

Editor: Jan Warren
Cover design: Joy Whitney and Elisa Hindman

for Neva

Contents

Acknowledgments

First off, I want to thank all of my "brothers on the wall." In Nehemiah, those early dads and fighters and builders were stationed on the wall around Jerusalem and they were each building up their own section of it. It has been good to work right alongside you men.

You have been my friends, my mentors, my encouragement and my example. In this book I quote a number of you as "a fellow dad," but you are much more than that. You are my heroes. Thanks for the 30-year conversation.

I hope I did it right.

I want to thank Brad Barrett for first pushing me to write this book. Only your strong encouragement made me even consider tackling something like this. Thanks for your help in reading it over, offering input and writing all of the discussion questions.

We wanted to write a practical book and you helped get it there.

I want to thank Jan Warren for her skillful help in editing. Years ago you turned my first efforts at writing into something much better. You still are amazing, gracious, and very good at what you do. Thank you so much. You deserve to stand before kings.

I also want to thank my children for letting me be open and honest about their lives, their strengths, their frustrations and their mistakes. You each are my delight. You are real cause for pride in my heart and collectively you are my very best work in this life. I am very thankful for the amazing hearts you show and for your courageous spirits. I know it hasn't always been easy living with me.

And last but not least, I want to thank my wife Neva for all of her faithful service, incredible patience and hard work. I have observed that it is "unto the Lord" first, but I also know that I have been a big recipient. You will not lose your reward. I have told you this often, but I just wanted to say it again: *You are the best thing that has ever happened to this country boy.* I appreciate your love, Nev.

Keep pressing,
Rick

Foreword

"After 24 years of following Christ, I have to admit that I have seen few exemplary "second-generation Christians." By that I mean, God-fearing believing children, who are the offspring of God-fearing parents. Although many Christian parents do love and fear God, seldom is the next generation quite as "hot" for God.

I see few even in the Bible. Think of King David. At least several of his sons didn't turn out so well, causing him and an entire nation grief. Think of Eli the prophet. His sons brought disgrace to the name of God.

Why? Why does this happen? On the one hand, these stories can discourage me and cause me to think that perhaps raising a godly second generation is a little like spinning the wheel on Wheel of Fortune. Simply hope I get lucky. But on the other hand, I wonder if there are commands and principles in the Word of God that I can turn to in order to find answers, answers that will work.

I also wonder if we have not looked hard enough to find living examples around us who really are being successful in their parenting.

If I have had any success as a father over the past seventeen years, it is largely based on the example of other dads who are succeeding in producing a hot second generation. And I know that their parenting has been based on a careful, prayerful following of the Scriptures.

Rick Whitney is one of those men in my life. He has not just talked the talk, he has walked the walk. For years, I have admired his heart and his faith, especially concerning his family. But what has truly sealed it for me is the fruit in his children's lives.

No doubt Rick would be quick to admit that he is not the perfect father, nor are his children perfect. But in his family I see something unusual, an unusual love, respect and devotion. Discipline, courage, and a strong work ethic.

A compassionate heart for the souls of others. A love for Christ.

His family is a rare commodity. Too rare.

But it doesn't have to be that way. As you read this book, ask yourself, "Am I following someone who has had genuine success in raising up a hot second-generation?"

- Brad Barrett, father, pastor, teacher, friend

Introduction

Now it seems like a long time ago. Over twenty-six years have passed since we had our little baby boy.

Actually he wasn't so little. Fourteen months old and chubby as a sumo wrestler - he was the light of our life. We loved him and thought the world of him. Like all new parents, we couldn't begin to describe what he meant to us. *But he was a handful!*

His behavior was often embarrassing. It was tough to have people over for dinner. Sometimes it was tough to go out in public, even to Wal-Mart. Often he didn't like what we were trying to teach him, and he let us know!

How embarrassing.

A few years went by and we had a baby girl. A cute, precious, little girl.

But one of my favorite memories of her, beyond her wonderful smile, was the time I trudged up the stairs when I heard her crying. I walked into the bedroom and there she was, standing up in her crib with each of her little hands firmly clenching a rail, her face perched on the top rail, shaking the bars of her "prison" with all of her might. She was angry, very angry, and let me know it as soon as she saw me.

As angry as a little girl can ever be, I guess.

And then we had another little girl.

Have you ever had a child who was so sensitive that if you just looked at her cross-eyed she would start blubbering? Her lower lip would quiver and her eyes would puddle at the drop of a hat. Well, that little girl grew up over the years and now leads with her heart, first and always.

And then years later, we had another child. (Having kids was becoming a habit!)

We had just come back from a trip to see the grandparents. The older three were in bed, but my fourth child was still up, since she had napped quite a bit in the car that afternoon. I was working through a pile of mail on my desk and asked this sweet, precious, little two-year-old girl to run a letter down to her mom.

She had been sitting on my lap up until this point, so I put her down, handed her the letter and told her to scoot. Whereupon, she immediately dropped the letter and said just as clearly as can be, "No!"

What followed was a frustrating, exhausting hour – for both of us.

Have you ever had your young son ride off with a few of his buddies on their bikes and then half an hour later get a phone call from a neighborhood grandmother? That neighbor has just seen your boy in her back yard near her hen house, with a bunch of eggs cradled in his T-shirt!

Have you ever had a child who could easily crash on the sofa and watch TV for whole days at a time and think nothing of it? A child who could then turn to you when you walk in the room and point this out, and answer, "Wha..a..a..a..t?" This one grew up and now likes to run everything. Would you like to know how we turned things around? I'd love to tell you.

Have you ever had a child who can sit in a room with two (or twenty-two) other people and quietly take it all in? She may never say a word and yet you know, deep down in her heart, that she is really scrutinizing everything, judging the whole, crazy circus swirling around her?

Eventually all seven of them all started growing up. (Thankfully, they do that just kind of naturally and fairly quickly.)

Then one day, one of those sweet, young angels turns to you at sixteen, puts her hands on her hips, and states fiercely, "Dad, sometimes I don't think you love me!" You see the fire in her eyes and know that what she really wants to say was, "Dad, I hate you!" What do you do? Well, we'd better know what to do.

These kinds of situations – where the rubber meets the road – are what parenting is all about. Do we have the right answers for these times? We will need answers desperately, if we are going to keep our sanity and help these kids grow into mature adults.

I want to get right into real life on the home front in this book. I want our stories to encourage you, and I believe they will.

Just how do you write a book on parenting? I'm not sure. I've never done it before.

Why even write a book on parenting you ask? Well, here's my reason for writing it:

I believe that God gave our movement – the Great Commission Association of Churches – a unique perspective on parenting. We recognize that all godly parenting must have an outward focus, a purpose that glorifies God. We believe that purpose is the advancement of the Great Commission in and through our marriages and our families.

That is why I am writing this book.

Many Christian parenting books and child-raising curriculums seem somewhat selfish. The unspoken assumption in many of them is that we can somehow train our kids and "save" them from our corrupt society, and yet ignore this lost world.

Our Lord addressed this selfish attitude when He said, "For whoever wishes to save his life shall lose it… " Our "life" obviously includes our marriages and our children.

Our Lord continued with, "But whoever loses his life for My sake and the gospel's shall save it." These Scriptures warn us that if all we care about is keeping our children and families safe, we are headed for heartache.

There are probably a hundred books on the topic of marriage and family down at your nearest bookstore. But I have yet to read one that recognizes that the advancement of God's Kingdom is the key to raising successful, Christian families.

Raising givers, not takers

Recently I read a column by Becky Hart in the <u>Rocky Mountain News</u> entitled, "Uber-parents turning out kids who are not so super." In her piece, she notes that many parents today are so child-focused and obsessed with their kids, that they are actually doing their kids a disservice. She quotes Patricia Dalton, a clinical psychologist and mother of three, who describes these parents as "uber-parents."

As Dalton puts it, these folks "decorate their children's rooms in stimulating colors, buy educational toys, forgo playpens and give baby massages. They sacrifice personal time, friendships and their own interests… and perhaps most important, they take every opportunity to build up their children's self-esteem."

She concludes, "Today's children may love themselves, but in the end the biblical 'Do unto others' is like a foreign language to them. They are takers, not doers or givers."

She proposes two reasons for this: 1) the smaller size of families and 2) our greater affluence here in America.

But whatever the reason, she confirms that it is possible to give too much attention to your kids. "Child-centered-ness can easily become child *idolatry*," she writes. Her remedy? "Uber-parents" need to get their children off the pedestal, for their sake and for the sake of their children.

Dalton goes on to suggest that families that are not so obsessively child-focused are probably happier. Those more balanced parents are, in her words, "certainly more likely to raise kids who will be individuals who care more about the needs and happiness of others."

Isn't that just what we are looking for with our children? Don't we all want to raise kids who are oriented towards others and involved in reaching out to this dying world?

We Christian parents can easily treat our children as idols. But God has given us the solution: an outward orientation. We need to get involved with our families in a great and noble cause, the advancement of His Kingdom.

Thankfully, God has given this vision of "families on a mission" to our association of churches. We believe this vision is vital to the ultimate success of our families. In the chapters that follow, I would like to share with you just how this vision can work itself out in practical ways within a real American family.

We will look at several other topics besides parenting. We will look at topics that relate to peace and purpose in our homes, God's vision for our marriages, the different roles of men and women in a family, and the over-arching, God-given duty and calling that God has entrusted to each of us in our homes.

We will discuss what I feel is critical for parents to know, understand, and appreciate about raising kids. I want to write about the main things that I have learned with my own "brood" and to share them, hopefully, with a little humor. I will cover the principles that we have taught many times to thousands of couples in over fifty churches during our weekend parenting seminars.

In his book <u>Halftime</u>, Bob Buford concluded that, "Men spend the first half of their life looking for success. They spend the last half of their life looking for significance." Might I again suggest that apart from success within our families, there is very little lasting significance to our lives.

These chapters are weighted heavily towards dads. It is an honor for me to talk to other dads. I hope that every mother who reads this book will find encouragement in what I say. But I am a father, and I have written much of this material for other fathers, for my fellow "brothers on the wall."

My prayer is that each of you will be built up as parents through this book. That you might have *stronger hearts* and *stronger willpower*. In the chapters that follow, I want to share my heart, my passion and my conviction that *every parent can succeed in raising great kids!*

- The first few chapters will deal with children under twelve and the first basic foundations that need to be established in their hearts.

- Then through the rest of this book we will deal with our youth who are now teenagers - maintaining good attitudes and imparting our vision to them.

As you read through each chapter (almost a collection of essays) and mull over the discussion questions, know that my first purpose in writing is that you would be deeply encouraged.

We all have questions. I pose several hundred and try to answer them. I thought about entitling this - <u>1001 Questions that Parents Ask</u>.

But when you finish reading, my prayer is that you will know the only question that really matters as a parent - and have an answer for it.

I have shared the following statement often, with all the passion I can muster, over and over again for over twenty years:

"I believe that the greatest need in becoming successful parents is to have strong hearts and strong willpower."

This is where we have to be at the end of the day, and I believe this book can help. So I hope you read it. I trust that you won't be disappointed.

Keep pressing,
Rick

1
Starting off on the Right Foot

"Ideally they should give you a couple of 'practice kids' before you have any for real. Sort of like bowling a few frames for free before you start keeping score. Let you warm up."

- Paul Reiser (from his book <u>Couplehood</u>)

Just how do we go about this business of child raising anyway? Does anyone *really* know what he's doing – or are we all just sort of out there on our own trying to wing it the best way we know how?

I have to be honest with you. Those weren't exactly the burning questions that Neva and I grappled with when we were first married. Actually, they were the farthest thing from our minds. But then we woke up one morning, looked at each other across the bed and suddenly realized that we weren't just married anymore – we were *parents*!

I don't know about you, but when we were first initiated into this mysterious club called parenthood, we didn't have much expertise to fall back on. We both came from relatively solid home backgrounds and we knew a few couples that we thought were pretty decent parents. But nothing prepared us for the reality of actually *being* parents!

Somehow, from the start we just sort of instinctively knew that our children were going to end up being our greatest source of joy on this earth. (Who knew, before that first little one came into your life, that you could be mesmerized for literally hours taking in all those different weird faces and sounds your baby makes? You didn't need to be a civil engineer to know that even the best day at the office couldn't begin to compete with the joys of baby Josh!)

I guess we all know deep down inside that our kids are well worth our best efforts when it comes to raising them and training them up "in the way that they should go." But where are the real, substantive answers to the complex and confusing issues we all face in trying to raise our kids right?

We had that same question as new parents. In fact, when it came to raising kids, Neva and I only knew one thing for sure – we wanted to do it right.

The last thing that we wanted was to get caught up in some child-raising fad that was making the talk show circuit – only to find out later that it didn't work. Instead, we wanted answers that had stood the test of time, principles that had actually been *proven to work* (what a concept, huh?) over and over down through history.

But whom should we listen to?

Will the real expert please stand up?

There are many self-proclaimed "experts" promoting many

schools of thought on childrearing. Undoubtedly the best known was and is Dr. Benjamin Spock.

Over fifty years ago, Dr. Spock basically told all of America: If you want to know how to raise your children, read my book. Many Americans, hungry for practical information on how to raise their kids right, did just that. His book Baby and Child Care, first published in 1946 (just in time for the baby boom), has been translated into 42 languages and has sold over 50 million copies. After the Bible, it is currently the world's best-selling non-fiction book!

It is no exaggeration to say that since World War II, literally millions of parents influenced by his ideas and theories have raised several generations of children "according to Spock."

Now, after millions of these kids have passed through adolescence, trooped off to college, gotten married and begun having their own children (and now grandchildren), Dr. Spock suddenly confessed a few years back, "I guess a lot of my assumptions were wrong."

What? The so-called expert on raising several entire generations of young people *guesses he was wrong?* Nice of him to tell us, but the fact is, it's too late. The damage has been done!

So who's right?

Whenever we hear anyone speaking on the topic of raising children – whether it's a TV star or a respected author in Parents magazine – we need to ask the following two questions:
1. Is this person right or wrong in what he's sharing?
2. Is there any resulting proof – or as we Christians might say, "fruit" – in the real world to validate his theories? In short, has it been proven to work?

(While we're on the subject, let me just say up front that before you take *my* word on anything related to raising your children, you need to ask these same two questions of me, too.)

So how do we determine whether someone is right or wrong? Obviously, we need some sort of standard or set of rules – one that we know always works – to use to evaluate any input we get on this crucial topic. Is there really such a thing – a set of principles that always works – that every child raising theory can be measured against?

If there is, it's vital that we know about it. After all, our children are priceless. We only go around once with our kids, and we can't afford to spend their impressionable, life-shaping years experimenting.

I don't want to tiptoe around this, so I'll just say it right out. *I base all of my child raising decisions on the Bible, specifically the book of Proverbs.*

For many centuries, in countless cultures and countries, among diverse peoples and languages, the instruction found in the book of Proverbs has been a guiding light to the successful personal and social development of millions of children. Countless great men and women of history are the product of its teaching.

The principles in the Bible work. They've been proven to work for almost 3,000 years, while Dr. Spock's now-defunct theories didn't even work for a single generation. The fact is, we shouldn't trust anyone's advice – no matter how knowledgeable or well intended – if it differs from the principles in the Bible.

Does it work?

There is a still a second question that you as a parent need to ask before you read this or any other book on child rearing, and the question is this: *What sort of results have you gotten applying the principles that you promote in your own family at home?*

In other words, does what you say actually work in the real

world? That's a great question. Because if what I teach in this book doesn't work in real life – in the nitty, gritty realities of everyday experience – then I shouldn't be pushing it and you shouldn't be reading it.

Pardon my digression, but that reminds me of a course I took in college called "Courtship and Marriage." I'll never forget the first day of class. My professor walked in and the first words out of her mouth were "I have been divorced three times, and now I'm married for the fourth time. I know what I am talking about."

She probably thought she knew her stuff, but I'd say she was a little confused.

Lots of folks have lots of opinions on lots of things. One vital credential that anyone who teaches about raising kids needs to have is this: proven results in his or her own immediate family. Every parent has the right to ask challenging questions of any teacher – especially someone teaching on the topic of child raising.

In order to answer that second question, we'll need to fast forward about 30 years. If you haven't noticed by now, Neva and I have a large family by today's standards – seven kids in all. Throughout this book you'll find lots of personal illustrations and stories about each of my family members – not only the good, but also the bad and the ugly. You can judge for yourself how we have dealt with the difficulties we've faced and whether or not we have "won" with each of our kids. But let me take just a moment at the outset to share with you briefly what I believe God has done in my children.

A look at the Whitney kids

My oldest four have each graduated from public high school and have all gone on to college. In high school they were involved in all kinds of clubs and activities. They were all involved in leading classmates to Christ and leading Bible studies in their high school.

They brought many friends to teen conferences and saw a lot happen for God in their school. Academically they all did very well, because we insisted that they work hard and they did.

In my experience with my kids, good academics is largely a product of hard work.

(I recognize that all children have different amounts of God-given, gray cells. Just like their moms and their dads. My kids all have different gifts and weaknesses, just like their parents. And sometimes it is more than just a weakness - there are genuine, physical and mental handicaps and limitations – all God given. As the Scriptures says, we are each fearfully and wonderfully made. And God has His purposes in making each of us so unique. Recognizing this reality, our Lord would want us to build individually into each one of our kids. We can't expect "cookie cutter" results. Yet we also can not accept a lack of specific, maybe God-limited effort – but genuine effort from each and every child, no matter what their strengths and weaknesses.)

We also told them that if they chose to go to college, they would need to prepare for it financially. And they did. At age eighteen, one by one, they each moved into the dorms and started living life "on their own dime."

I am very proud of how they have each worked their way through college. There is nothing wrong with helping your kids with college expenses, but our kids earned scholarships, grants, etc. and then began to work as Resident Assistants.

They have plugged their way through college.

When my oldest first became an RA, there was very little going on at Colorado State University spiritually speaking, but things soon changed. The student group that had just a handful of students when Josh first arrived now boasts several hundred students.

Our kids have led and multiplied literally dozens of small groups and have seen dozens of students join them as RA's on many different dorm floors.

They have also been very involved in leadership within their college church at CSU. As one pastor put it, "A case could be made that there wouldn't *be* a 'Rock' apart from the Whitney kids."

My oldest two have now graduated from college and are married. Josh has his Master's degree and is married to Krista. Mandy is married to Tom Brown, who is a campus staff worker. Krista and Tom are two very special people. Neva and I are blessed by both of our children's choice of a life partner.

My third, Joy, is just beginning her Master's program. Grace, my fourth and youngest college student, has finished her second year, and is an RA and leads out in her campus small group.

Mike has just graduated from high school and is headed off to college soon. He also received many awards while in high school and was also a pretty good wrestler.

His two younger sisters round out our brood – Jessica will be a senior in high school and our youngest daughter, Rebecca, a sophomore.

We have, by the grace of God, been able to instill a servant's attitude in every one of their hearts. And we are thankful for this blessing.

They each work hard at their academics and are influential for Christ, regardless of their age. I believe you can train leadership into a child and we have built leadership into all of them. They have all served as presidents and leaders and captains in many different circles – in school and out of school, in church, in 4-H, in athletics, you name it.

All seven of our children have been actively involved with us in several different church plants and have rubbed shoulders with many other pastors, leaders and youth workers. They have spoken at conferences, led spring break outreaches and summer ministry projects, and have routinely led out in a variety of ways in a number of different situations with different leaders over them.

You could check with the leaders and parents in any one of several churches they have been involved in and ask just how our kids have done. I'm sure they would give you an honest appraisal.

As parents, we are duly proud of what our children have tackled and accomplished. But the main reason we are proud of their accomplishments is because we see the hard work and proven character that lies behind them.

Whatever the future holds

With now just two kids left in high school, Neva and I have a quiet confidence about one thing in particular. If the Lord were to take us out of this world today, we know that our kids are on a sort of spiritual "autopilot" (in a good way) when it comes to their direction in life. That is, they are securely locked on course. We are absolutely sure that if we were suddenly removed from the picture today, our kids would all go on to make good choices and do well in life.

They'll go on to college, they'll graduate, they'll marry well and, best of all, they'll serve the Lord for the rest of their lives. This isn't wishful thinking on our part. We have seen it happening consistently for many years now.

They look out for each other. They correct each other. They are each on the right path. This might sound like bragging and I guess it is. But I am bragging on God.

We are certainly not perfect parents. Far from it. But, by His grace, He has helped us to be good parents. He has guided us in raising these seven champions, who are our pride and joy and our very best work in this life. We are truly grateful for their hearts for us and for our Lord.

My summary in a sentence? My basis for all I will write about in this book is the Scriptures – and the proof that the principles I'm about to share work in real life is found in my kids.

Chapter 1 – Discussion Questions

1. What can you do to learn more from Proverbs about parenting?

2. What other sources have you looked to? Do they support Proverbs' wisdom?

3. Do you have other parents to emulate who are enough "*ahead of you,*" both in the age of their children and in successfully training them?

2
The Basics

"Call them rules or call them limits, good ones, I believe, have this in common: They serve reasonable purposes... and they are an expression of loving concern."

- Mister Rogers

"Establishing limits, structure, rules, and expectations takes self-confidence on the part of parents. Parents need to recognize that they are the legitimate authority figures in their households and feel secure in that role."

- Karen Levine

"Children can't make their own rules and no child is happy without them. The great need of the young is for authority that protects them ... and that builds some solid ground they can stand on for the future."

- Leontine Young

In general, the Bible stresses two important dynamics that are sadly missing between most parents and children in America today. I consider them to be the most basic building blocks of successful parenting. Both are outlined repeatedly in the book of Proverbs. Let's take a closer look at these two crucial principles.

Trust, the bottom line
The first dynamic that the Bible stresses is trust. That's right – simple trust. Trust between a father and his son. Trust between a mother and her daughter.
Ask yourself, "Does each of my children trust me? If not, why not?"
Trust is a two-way street. It takes time to develop. Have we given our children the time that's necessary to build trust? It isn't just the quality of the time we give them that builds trust. Nor is it the quantity of time. In actuality, it's both. We need to spend meaningful time with our child – and plenty of it – if we want to develop a relationship that's grounded in mutual trust.
That reminds me of an incident that took place in the Whitney household a while back (actually, quite a while back, as you'll be able to tell from the central activity in the story).

One night, my kids and I were playing hide-and-seek. Actually, it was a variation on the game. I was pretending to be a bear and the kids were hiding upstairs.

*Now when I'm prowling and growling and all of my kids
are running and screaming and laughing, it gets to be a zoo
pretty quickly. Needless to say, the house was pandemonium.
As I lumbered through one of the kids' bedroom doors on
all fours, I happened to catch sight of Gracie, my four-year-
old, hiding as quiet as a mouse in an especially shadowy corner
of her darkened room. Her eyes were open wide and her hands
were clamped over her mouth like she was stifling a scream.*

I let out my very best bloodcurdling growl.

*To my surprise, she just stood up, marched right over to
me and threw her arms around my neck. Apparently she had
had enough of the game.*

"Weren't you afraid, Gracie?" I asked her.

"No, silly," she answered. "You're Daddy."

*I hugged her back. It was a little thing, but it warmed my
heart. She trusted Dad more than she was afraid of any ol'
bear in the dark.*

Like my daughter Gracie, all of our children have entrusted us
with their hearts at a very young age. It's important for us to realize
what an awesome responsibility we have to protect that sacred
trust. We parents, especially the dads among us, need to remember
how easy it is to crush their tender spirits. Their simple, trusting
attitude should compel us to mindfully focus our energies on
maintaining that mutual trust.

Rules to live by

Once we've built a foundation of trust and security, the second
dynamic that the Bible says we need to grapple with is developing
consistent rules for our children to live by.

Just as an adult needs a touchstone for his life, a child also
needs to see clearly where the boundaries are. What I mean is

this, a young child needs to know what is right and what is wrong and how to behave accordingly. Eventually society will lay down guidelines for a child's life, but we parents are the first "law-givers" our children ever experience.

So what are the rules? Here are a few of the first rules that a child needs to learn: be gentle, tell the truth, obey. And of course, there's that all-time classic: understanding the meaning of the word "No."

As parents, we're continually adding to these guidelines as our children mature and it's only right for us to do this. In fact, if we want our children to be healthy – physically, socially and emotionally – it is our duty to establish some sense of order and structure in their lives. It is our responsibility as parents to provide them with "guardrails" on the road of life, so to speak – both to identify where the road is and to keep them from veering off of it.

While children need the security that boundaries, rules and discipline provide, have you ever noticed that they seldom request these things for themselves? In fact, only once in over two decades of helping hundreds of parents have I ever heard of a child who – on his own, mind you – recognized that he needed to be corralled and trained. Only once! Let me tell you briefly about that memorable day.

It happened a few years back to a young mother who had twin boys. They were a handful, to say the least. They were about eight years old and full of incredible energy. Live wires, 24/7!

But one day, the boys came up to their mother – this is the absolute truth – and said, "Mom, we think we need some discipline."

She was absolutely flabbergasted! After she recovered from the initial shock, however, her motherly instincts immediately kicked into overdrive. " Just what have they been up to that would make them say that?" she wondered.

We may never know this side of heaven what possessed those young boys to *ask* for discipline. But we can make one very good assumption: our kids won't come right out and ask us to limit their freedom. We're going to have to take the initiative not only to develop and communicate our family "rules of the road" to our kids, but also to consistently enforce them – for our kids' own good (as well as our own sanity!).

"It is better for you to cry now than for me to cry later."

- Old Italian saying

The book of Proverbs clearly states that "a child who gets his own way brings shame to his mother." If we are slack in giving our children guidelines and just let them have their own way, it will only bring us shame.

A few years ago, I was visiting in a home where the parents allowed their little son to literally do as he pleased. They had put away all of the breakables (including all of the lamps) and had hidden all the dangerous items (including the kitchen knives) and given the little boy the run of the place. He strutted around like Son of King Kong.

I'd heard other parents tell similar stories of quasi-legendary families and children that they knew, but it wasn't until I saw the crayon marks on literally every wall in the house that I finally believed that someone would actually buy in to such a permissive child raising theory.

How short sighted! Eventually the kid will need to learn not to color on the walls – if not by the time he is five, at least by the time he is twenty. Sooner or later, if he hopes to function in society, he's going to need to learn some basic rules of behavior.

"Unfortunately, children don't come already trained, and whether we like it or not, they will sometimes develop habits and attitudes [that] we need to train them out of."

- Ian Grant

Parents, it is primarily our responsibility to provide rational boundaries for our children. The responsibility does not belong to our child or to his older siblings or to his playmates. It does not belong to grandma or his teacher or his pastor or his babysitter or the lady behind us in the grocery line. It does not even belong to society.

It belongs to good old Mom and Dad.

Of course, every parent will define these boundaries somewhat individually, but the standards of good conduct and character for children that are outlined in Proverbs are an excellent starting point.

Honesty, diligence, faithfulness, a value for hard work – the Book lays them all out in great detail. If you want kids who are honest, who enjoy a job well done, who are courageous and who have an open, cheerful spirit, then train them in the principles of Proverbs. It isn't a large book, but it is literally jammed with practical how-to's for all of us to follow.

Later we will talk about the "whys?" I don't mean answering those defiant "whys," where our kids have hands on their hips and a glare in their eyes. And I am not talking about asking why, just as a delaying tactic on their part.

But there are honest "whys" that do come up. When kids have had rules, but later have rebelled, usually it is traced to one of two things. We did not insist upon heart-felt, complete obedience on their part, when they were young. Or later we did not give them honest, Biblical reasons for those rules.

Sometimes children have rebelled in part because they have been given the rules, but not the heart or spirit behind it. So we will tackle some of those juicy conversations later. But I honestly believe that often children rebel late, because parents did not capture their hearts through careful, clear instruction and a consistent example.

I'd encourage you to discuss these two principles – the need for trust and the need for rules – together as parents. Then evaluate your own situation. Is there warmth in your family? Is there order?

God wants our families to have both and He's given us the roadmap. But it's up to us to read His Book and find out just what He has in mind. And here is the best part: He not only tells us where we need to be, He also shows us how to get there!

Chapter 2 – Discussion Questions

On trust:
1. Do your children trust you? In what areas or circumstances do they trust you? In what ones don't they? What are things that would prove or disprove your answer?

2. How can you build that trust?

3. Is there anything you have done or said (or *not* done or said) that has hurt their trust in you? What will you do to re-establish that trust?

On rules:

1. How difficult is it for you to establish rules? How difficult is it for you to be consistent with those rules?

2. Do you and your spouse differ on the specific rules and your consistency with them? (Discuss this with your spouse.)

3. Is it hard or easy to say "No", and then stick with it? Why?

3
First Things First

"*Raising children is part joy and part guerrilla warfare.*"

– Ed Asner

I had just pulled into the grocery store parking lot and had hopped out of the car to go in and get a few things for my wife, Neva. Parked a few cars down was a young mother and her little boy. It was a hot, sweltering afternoon and you could tell this mom was pretty hot under the collar herself. "Please get in the car," she said sternly. I could hear her repeating it – over and over and over again – as I walked into the store.

Twenty minutes later I came out with my groceries and she was still there – standing over him sweating, asking him to get in the car. She was clearly upset and so was her little boy.

But nothing had happened.

Every parent I have ever met loves his or her kids. Though there are moments when we get pretty frustrated, deep down we still love them. But the frustrations, the doubts and the confrontations all add up over time and can make us feel anxious and defeated as moms and dads.

That is why we need strong hearts and a constant strength of will if we are going to raise these kids right. So much hangs in the balance. Not just our own daily peace of mind, but an entirely separate, unique life – our child's. No amount of success in this world can make up for our loss if we fail in our own homes and with our kids.

I know that no home is perfect. As long as people are human, there will always be sins and setbacks. But if we continually fail with our kids inside our homes, then our lives will be miserable – no matter how much money we make or how many people applaud us outside our homes.

Far and away the most important foundation stone we need to place in the hearts of our sons and daughters is an understanding of, and appreciation for, obedience.

But first we need to value obedience as parents. We need to deeply esteem obedience as the foundation upon which all character is built. There is no real character apart from obedience.

Our Lord is the one Who first asked each of us, "How can you say that you love Me, if you will not do what I say?"

I want to tell you a story of how God first got hold of me in the area of appreciating obedience as a parent.

Neva and I had been married about six years, I was pastoring a church in Iowa and we had our first little boy, Josh. I thought he was the most beautiful little boy I had ever seen, but I also knew that at times he was just plain out of control. In short, he was a pickle!

When Josh was about fifteen months old, I was invited to a conference for pastors up in the mountains of Colorado. Each pastor was encouraged to bring his wife and family with him. Neva and I were looking forward to the time to see old friends, make new friends and listen to some great messages.

But we were also dreading it.

We knew without a doubt that Josh would be a handful and that we would be embarrassed. So we came up with a devious scheme to cover up our inadequacy as parents – we decided to camp out.

Now Neva and I never camp. We hate to camp. We are country folks. Only city folks like camping. So even though everyone else stayed in quaint little cabins or in the ski lodge, Neva and I toughed it out in a tent with a toddler.

Here I was, a leader in the church, and I was miserable and embarrassed. Why? Because I didn't first value my own obedience to what God clearly had to say on the subject of child-rearing. In Proverbs 13:24, the Lord specifically says, "He who spares his rod hates his son, but he who loves him disciplines him diligently." Up to this point I thought I had been obeying God and His Bible in my life. But I suddenly realized that I wasn't obeying God **as a parent**.

I just didn't want to spank Josh. He was too cute. (I didn't know any one else who wanted to spank him either. You can't seem to hire these things out!)

Once you've been a parent of several kids, you know that spanking is really no big deal. But it sure was a big deal to me, because I just didn't want to do it! I thought I could get around this verse and many others like it. And so Neva and I *and our big "bundle of joy" camped out all that week, until God finally broke through to my miserable heart.*

He just seemed to kind of whisper the same thing over and over to me:

"Rick, do you trust Me? Will you trust that I know how to help you raise your boy? Will you believe that what I have written is for your boy's own good? Would you please recognize that spanking is not 'the end of the world'? Will you obey me, Rick? Will you do what I've said?"

So I decided to obey God.

I will never forget that first time I spanked Josh. It was pretty emotional for me. But after I had instructed him and spanked him and comforted him, I leaned back against a pine tree there on the mountainside and Josh just fell asleep peacefully in my arms. And then I started crying.

So God knew what He was talking about. Josh was going to be okay. Things were going to work out. He wasn't going to become an axe murderer. For the first time, I relaxed a bit as a parent.

Amazing, isn't it? I thought my son's obedience was the big issue that week – but it was really good old Dad's obedience. When I finally relented and went ahead and tried it God's way, things immediately started getting better.

I will never forget that lesson. Obedience is key and we need to first appropriate it as parents before we can instill it in our children.

At times, you just have to do what God says, whether you feel like it or not. There is no way to get around it.

Our whole society is trying to learn this ... and failing miserably. Let's face it, we normally only do things if they <u>feel</u> good or if they <u>feel</u> right. But if we want to win when it comes to parenting, then we have to trust in God and <u>do</u> what He says, whether it <u>feels</u> good or right or not.

Once we step out and obey – even if we don't feel like it – our emotions almost always get in line. He has written in the book of Psalms that if we follow the way of His commands, He will "enlarge our hearts" (Psalm 119:32). Our hearts follow our actions. And God's peace follows it all, calming our fears and giving us renewed confidence that His ways work.

If these kind of lessons aren't learned at two, four and six years of age, then they are only compounded at twelve, fourteen and sixteen.

We really are foolish if we think we can just talk to them, stall them, avoid the confrontation, maybe placate them by doing that good old "song and dance." No matter how much fun we have with our children, there will be many times where confrontation is called for.

Discipline that leads to an understanding of the benefits and blessings of obedience – starting in our own lives – is the solid foundation upon which we can begin to build our child's character.

"Nothing I have ever done has given me more joys and rewards, than being a father to my five."

- Bill Cosby

Chapter 3 – Discussion Questions

1. How do you relate to the humorous (or not-so-humorous) quote, *"Raising children is part joy and part guerrilla warfare."*? Which have you experienced more of - joy or warfare?

2. As stated in the chapter, "I thought my son's obedience was the big issue that week – but it was really good old Dad's obedience." Is there any area of obedience in your role as a parent that is at issue?

3. Read Proverbs 13:24. How does "the rod" relate to your child's obedience? If you have used the rod only a little or not at all, what inhibits you from using it? If you have used it, what benefits have you seen? Discuss this with your spouse.

4
Lighting Fires

"Pay close attention to yourself and to your teaching; for as you do this, you will insure salvation, both for yourself and for those who hear you."

-1 Timothy 4:16

Whether you've been a parent for just a few months or for many few years, we both know that it takes more than a little energy. It takes a tremendous amount of emotional energy and raw fortitude of soul. And there is only one way that I know for a parent, no matter how dedicated, to get the spiritual strength he needs.

Parents, we must be in the Word!

If we as Christian parents want to do a great job with our kids, we first need to make sure that we ourselves are walking closely with the Lord. If we aren't building and cultivating our own relationships with the God of all parents, we honestly don't have a prayer, or much of a chance to win.

So early in this book I wanted to share the following story to strongly encourage each of us to carve out time to be personally ignited by God.

I had the day off. We lived out East and it was late in the fall and the kids and I decided to spend the day picking up downed branches in the woods out back and piling them up to burn. So we all bundled up and started gathering sticks and limbs and building our stack. The more we got into our work, the bigger the pile grew. By the time it started getting dark, we had quite a heap.

The kids pleaded with me to light it that night, but it had been raining for over a week, which made for one pretty soggy pile of rotten wood. I told them that we needed to let the woodpile dry out a bit and light it bright and early some Saturday morning when we could watch it through the day and make sure it burned safely.

A few weeks went by before we got back to the woodpile.

It had rained a bit over those weeks, but I thought the pile looked like it had dried out some. (Actually, it had dried out just a little along the top edges. The bulk of the wood was still damp, as we were soon to find out.)

I got some gasoline, doused the pile, had the kids stand back, and tossed on a lighted match.

Woomph!!

The pile went up like a ball of fire. Literally! Everything crackled for a minute, then the fire receded and died out.

Gas, match, woomph!! Gas, match, woomph!! I repeated the routine several times, with my kids squealing and loving every minute of it. It sure was impressive to throw the gas on and see the flames leap up 10 or 15 feet, but the pile wasn't starting to burn at all. Except for a few singed sticks of wood along the edges, the woodpile looked as sodden as ever.

I decided to change tactics. Inside the shed was some old scrap lumber that wasn't good for much of anything, so I grabbed an armful and a hatchet from the toolbox and split it up into a small pile of kindling. Then I laid this little heap of white pine along the edge of my great, big, soggy pile of fallen timber and lit it carefully. In a few minutes I had a small fire going, but my little flames seemed so hopeless up against that tall soggy stack of apathy.

My new fire was so pitifully small compared to the former inferno that my kids' quickly lost interest and wandered off down to the creek to play.

Pretty soon my small kindling fire was burning steadily enough to pull a few pieces of wet timber carefully down on top of it. You could hear the wood hissing and steaming as the little fire underneath slowly burned off the damp edges and then began attacking the heart of the wood.

I had some projects going in the shed, but I stopped occasionally to stick my head out the door and see how that meager, little blaze was doing. It did just fine – slowly burning off the water in its portion of the large, wet pile of wood, and then slowly heating up the whole stack. All morning the woodpile hissed and hissed, giving off thick white smoke.

When I came back after lunch, I noticed that the smoke was starting to clear.

By three o'clock that afternoon the whole tall pile was finally burning cleanly – no more hissing, very little smoke, just a tremendous crackling and a whole lot of heat. It was just like a roaring furnace. It was so hot we couldn't stand closer than 40 feet away!

Throughout that Saturday, as I was working in the shed and keeping one eye on the fire, I was thinking about an article that I needed to write.

I wanted to talk to you fathers, who work hard and are responsible for the many, many lives in our families. I believed that the Lord had given me one verse that He wanted me to share, but I wasn't sure just how He wanted me to share it till that Saturday when I burned that pile of wet wood.

As leaders in each of our families, we can all identify with Paul when he spoke of the burden of caring for people. Nothing brings us more joy than to see the people whom God has entrusted to our care happy and growing in the Lord. Nothing concerns us more than seeing our families tired in spirit.

But how do we lead them? How do we light up their hearts?

Christians can seem to be soggy and listless at times, just like that wood.

What can we do to see them fired up? *What can we do to fire ourselves up?*

God has given us an encouraging word, like He always does. He has shown us how to genuinely affect our families and the people in our lives.

In 1 Timothy 4:16, the Lord says,

"Pay close attention to yourself and to your teaching; for as you do this, you will insure salvation, both for yourself and for those who hear you."

As I read this verse, I was struck by the very first words: *"Pay close attention to yourself."* What does it mean to pay attention to yourself? What are we to pay attention to? Obviously, we are not to be self-centered. The Bible never encourages us to live for ourselves. God knows that selfishness will never be satisfied. So He must be talking about something else.

When Paul exhorted Timothy to pay attention to himself, it

was really so that Timothy could be a better servant to the people in his charge. Paul told Timothy to take pains with certain personal areas in his own soul so that he might bless others.

What were these areas that Timothy was to be absorbed with? Paul said that it was the simple, everyday things of this Christian life that were critical – not only to Timothy's personal *spiritual heat*, but ultimately to the well-being and *spiritual heat* of all of Timothy's kinsmen.

Specifically, he was told to persevere in good speech, correct conduct, genuine love, heroic faith and simple purity. (Yes, I added the adjectives so that you will slow down on these words and not just read right through them.)

Speech, conduct, love, faith and purity. These were the areas that Timothy was to take pains with. If he did this, Paul knew that Timothy's fire would burn and spread to the rest of the people around him.

"It only takes a spark to get a fire going" goes a line to an old song. Well, that song is true – if the wood is dry and ready to burn. But rarely is this the case.

So, what should we do?

We can throw gasoline on the wood. It may flare up for a season, but does it really start to burn? Usually not.

However, if there is just a little, tiny fire that is actually burning — and burning steadily *in our own heart* — eventually every member of our family will be in genuine danger of being genuinely fired up!

It starts with us, men. It starts with us, women. It starts with us, parents. It always has and it always will. *"Pay close attention... you will insure salvation... for yourself... and for those who hear you."* *"Those who hear you"* are first our families, and then our churches.

This is God's direction for us today. This is His formula for lighting a fire – first in one heart, then in one family, and then in a whole congregation.

Robert Murray McCheyne, a great man of God who lived over a hundred years ago, once said, *"Above all, cultivate your own spirit. A word spoken by you when your conscience is clear and your heart full of God's Spirit, is worth 10,000 words spoken in unbelief and sin."*

Do we believe this? Deep down in our hearts, do we believe this?

Personal integrity and personal purpose – *personal fire* – are the only things that will genuinely move people over the long haul.

Any leader and any parent can learn how to push the right emotional buttons and get the quick, easy "woomph" with people. But will there be a fire on Monday morning?

God promises that there will be, if we *"pay close attention – first to ourselves."*

Chapter 4 - Discussion Questions

1. How often do you find your heart soggy like the woodpile? What "douses the wood" in your life? (Read Matthew 13:22-23.)

2. How will you regularly *"pay closer attention"* to your speech, conduct, love, faith, and purity? How will this change in you affect your parenting?

5
What does it really mean to obey?

Let's face it – parenting is hard! It takes incredible courage coupled with an incredible, everyday kind of strength to succeed as a parent. We all can use a big dose of encouragement in this challenging work. In fact, I have yet to meet a single dad or mom who couldn't benefit from being built up in their role as parents.

The following questions touch on the kinds of issues we all face every day as parents, the kind of questions we address in detail in our parenting seminars. I think you'll find these ten questions to be very helpful in practically evaluating the "obedience quotient" in your own household. And they remind us how difficult our work is.

1. Do you find yourself frequently getting angry or impatient with your child when he or she disobeys you?

2. Wives, are you relieved when your husband comes home from work because then you can hand over the child discipline problems to him? (Husbands, does your wife do this often? If so, what do you think about that?)

3. Do you hesitate to invite people to your home because you know that the children might not be well behaved, that they might actually embarrass you?

4. Do you dread taking your children to the grocery store or to Wal-Mart, because you know that they will demand that you buy them something and eventually wear you down, that they will "make a scene?"

5. Do you fear in your heart that you really can't trust your child to act correctly when left on his own, with others, or with his peers?

6. Do you often find yourself exhausted and the house in disarray from dealing with your child(ren), whether they are toddlers or teens?

7. Do you feel that the neighbor children and/or your children's friends – whether they are seven or seventeen – control your family's schedule more than you would like?

8. Are you often in a quandary, not knowing how to respond to your child and his many different requests?

9. Do you find that your relationship with your mate suffers because of the daily demands of dealing with your children?

Does it cause a lot of tension and fighting between you both?

10. Do you blame your mate for your problems with the children?

Where do you find the solutions for all of the sticky issues raised in the questions above? Well, take heart, moms and dads, because the solution to all of these issues begins with one basic thing: the proper foundation established in the heart of each of our kids.

That proper foundation is obedience.

There are three aspects of obedience that we need to understand when we're talking about obedience with our children. (By the way, God wants us big people to understand these aspects of obedience in our own lives, too!)

I call them "The Three C's." Ask yourself:

1. Is the obedience *cheerful*?
2. Is the obedience *complete*?
3. Is the obedience *quick*?

(Okay, okay, I know – actually they're two C's and a Q. But you can remember them as "The Three C's" because they all sound alike ☺!)

It's pretty simple really. If we grumble and complain, it isn't *cheerful* obedience. If we only do the job halfway, it isn't *complete* obedience. And if we always delay and procrastinate, it isn't *quick* obedience. After all, God wants our obedience today, not later or tomorrow.

These three C's apply to everything – whether it's picking up toys, making a bed, mowing the lawn, or helping out at church.

This is where the Lord sets the bar when He talks to us about healthy, Christian obedience. He sets a pretty high standard, I admit, but it's something to shoot for and something we can attain more often than not if we put our minds to it.

I haven't always had this figured out, guys. If you don't believe me, you may talk to my wife. But I am here to tell you that it will pay off, if you will just stick with it.

"Those who are mostly consistent must use the switch too often. Those who are always consistent, come to almost never need the switch."

- Mike Pearl

The right tool for the job

Our words and our example are two of the most important tools that God has given us as parents. And the tool of discipline falls right in line behind them. Now every good tool has a purpose and the purpose of discipline is to train us in the benefits of healthy, open, honest, joyful obedience. Discipline – and I'm talking about spanking in the case of younger children – is just one of many tools in our parental tool kit, but it's an important tool and one that can produce amazing results.

Let me share an example:

We had been visiting the grandparents over Christmas and had just spent a long day driving back to our place in Maryland. Our three older children were tired when we got home, so we sent them right to bed.

However our youngest daughter, who was about two years old at the time, had been napping all the way across Pennsylvania. So she was up with Neva and me while we were putting things away and generally getting settled back in.

She was sitting on my lap at my desk as I sorted the mail

when I came across a letter that I knew Neva would enjoy. So I set Gracie down and asked her to run the letter down to her mom in the kitchen.

She smiled up at me with those great big eyes, looked down at the letter in her little hands, dropped the letter on the carpet, looked back up at me and said, "No!"

I almost laughed.

I said, "Honey, maybe you didn't understand daddy. Run this letter down to your mom, would you please?"

I put the letter back in her hands. She looked at the letter, dropped it on the carpet again, looked up at me and said again, just as clearly as she could, "No!"

So I went ahead and spanked her. She didn't need more reasoning. She didn't need a sermonette. She understood.

A lot of parents have told me over the years, "Spanking just doesn't seem to work for us." Well, I'm here to say that spanking *does* work – if you're committed to God's principle of discipline. You have to recognize that spanking is a healthy tool, a godly tool, a special tool in our parenting toolkit that God has specifically given us to help us in raising our kids.

When you spank, do you spank sort of haphazardly – you know, just a few quick noncommittal swats, just enough to get your child good and mad?

Don't do that. When we begin spanking the child is usually first shocked, then outraged, followed quickly by anger and resistance. A few swats will just get them worked up and in a rage.

You'll short-circuit the training process if you just spank them a couple times. It is much better to keep spanking your child until you can sense – and even see and hear – a certain "yielding" in his spirit and posture and crying. Remember, you are not spanking him to blow off steam – you are spanking him for the purpose of training him.

The Lord Himself is committed to this very purpose in our own lives as adults. In Hebrews 12:6 it says, *"For those whom the Lord loves, He disciplines."* God disciplines us as adults for our own good, to train us. His discipline is one way that He demonstrates His love for us.

In the same way, we need to discipline our children for their own good, to train them to be obedient. Our commitment to disciplining our children for their own good is one way we love our children "as God has loved us."

Now, back to the story.

So I spanked her and then comforted her and then set her back down and handed her the letter.

Now this is very important, parents. We need – at that very moment – to go right back to what we are trying to train them to do. It isn't obedience if we don't do what our Father tells us to do; nor is it obedience if our children don't do what we tell them to do.

"Gracie, run this letter down to your mom."
She looked at it once again, looked up at me, dropped the letter and said, "No!"
I didn't laugh. I was not even tempted to laugh now.

At times like these, a lot of things run through our minds as parents.

We wonder if we were clear enough. We wonder if little Johnny understands us or is even capable of understanding us. This same child was so brilliant just half an hour ago, but now we are questioning whether he or she can even understand the basic principles of communication. We wonder if some mysterious sort of neurological "brain freeze" has occurred. We wonder if we should chalk it up to demonic influences.

Don't. It ain't the devil.

Maybe Bill Cosby runs through our minds. Remember those immortal words on his TV show? *"I brought you into this world, and I can take you out!"*

Anyway, I spanked her again. Went through the same process. Comforted her. Wiped away her tears. Set her back down. Again she said, "No!"

And back and forth we went. For quite awhile.

I don't want you to miss my point here. My spanking is really not the issue. And her crying and my comforting her again and again is really not the issue either. The issue is obedience. The issue is training.

All of our spanking can be for naught, if we aren't dead serious about training and seeing change in our children. *Dear parent, we are not talking about talking – we are talking about training.*

Eventually I set her down, handed her the letter and asked her to run it down to her mom. And this time she did, bouncing down the stairs and delivering the letter to Neva like she had thought of it herself. Then she raced back upstairs and jumped back into my lap again. All smiles. Everything was fine.

Cheerful obedience. Complete obedience. Quick obedience. A right understanding of obedience isn't just good for the "hereafter." It's critical for the health of our soul and our body in the here and now. Being slow to obey can actually hurt us and prove dangerous to our well being. Let me illustrate.

Years ago, when my oldest boy was about four, he and I used to go outside after supper and bounce a basketball back and forth. I would sit on the front steps of our little house in Florida and he would take up a position on the sidewalk out front. I would bounce the ball to him and he would bounce it back to me. Then he would back up a few steps and we'd continue our game.

We bounced that ball most every night, hundreds of times.

One evening, I accidentally bounced the ball over his head and he turned and ran for it. I was kind of daydreaming at the time, but when I glanced up I saw what every father dreads in his worst nightmare — I saw my little boy running for the ball, headed right into the path of an oncoming car.

I jumped up and yelled, "Josh, stop!!"

He froze.

The ball went right under the front wheels of the car as it screeched to a halt.

My immediate thoughts were how very thankful I was that I had taught him to obey me quickly – not grudgingly or slowly or later. And how very thankful I was that he had learned to respond to my words – not my pleading or my whining or my nagging, just my simple words.

Okay, does all this make sense? Do you think you have an emotional handle on the importance of cheerful, complete and quick obedience? Have you made some progress, by the grace of God, and your children are responding? Do you believe that you've instilled some fairly good habits in their lives? Is there some element of peace in your home?

Then get ready. Buckle on your chinstrap.

Because when your son or daughter hits those middle years and the teen years – your work is just beginning!

Much too often, I have seen families that are sweet and solid when the kids are young turn into a war zone later on. And it's often because the parents assumed that if they did everything right in the beginning when the kids were little, things would just sort of take care of themselves in the later years. Nothing could be farther from the truth. We need to continue to emphasize cheerful, complete and quick obedience all through the teenage years!

Often we talk about "releasing" our sons and daughters when they are teens. Do not, I repeat, <u>do not release them too early</u>. And do not release them from these simple habits of cheerful, complete and quick obedience, whether they are seven or seventeen.

Sadly I have known several couples that, in my opinion, had done a good job with the little kids. But then naively they let things drift. Often they were shocked when more attitudes came out later when the kids were twelve or fifteen. Now that the kids were taller and bigger, suddenly the folks didn't know what to do.

I think they did know, but I believe they just didn't want to deal with it.

It is one thing when a five-year old resists our instructions. But it is quite another thing when a teenager, often taller than us, talks back. The teen usually says a whole lot. Or sometimes nothing. But either way it is harder for us parents.

We need to stay the course! We need to stay engaged! We need to keep training! We must! So much hangs in the balance.

"I believe that the greatest need for being a successful parent, it to have strong hearts and strong willpower."

Keep it simple

In closing, I'd like to encourage you not to forget the importance of keeping things simple. Don't make training and discipline too complicated. Heart issues and disobedience rarely are. We're not talking rocket science here. As a case in point, I'd like to let Ruth Bell Graham tell you in her own words how she kept child training simple and practical.

Here's a brief, somewhat tongue-in-cheek excerpt from her book It's My Turn:

Dear Journal,

Every parent should read at least one good book on dog training. Odd how, in a day when children are notoriously disobedient, dog training and obedience classes are increasing in popularity. Basically the rules are simple:

1. *Keep commands simple and at a minimum. One word to a command and always the same word. Come. Sit. Stay. Heel. Down. No. (I talk my children dizzy at times.)*

2. *Be consistent.*

3. *Be persistent. Follow through. Never give a command without seeing that it is obeyed.*

4. *When the dog responds correctly, praise him. (Not with food. Remember, don't reward children materially for doing well. Your praise should be enough.)*

It is a fine kettle of fish when our dogs are better trained than our children.

For further study:

On the resource page of our Great Commission Northwest Dads web site (gcnwdads.com), is an excellent article on child discipline entitled Under Loving Command. Authored by Pat Fabrizio, it is also available as a booklet.

I have handed out literally hundreds of copies for over 25 years at our weekend parenting seminars. I recommend it.

Chapter 5 – Discussion Questions

1. Discuss the ten questions at the beginning of the chapter with your spouse. Then discuss them with another couple who will be able to help.

2. Concerning the aspects of obedience (cheerful, complete and quick), how are you doing in your own life? In other words, what example are you setting? In order to get the best picture of how you are doing, ask your spouse or even one of your children how the "CCQ" obedience is in our own life.

3. Have your children made progress in "CCQ"? If yes, have you praised them for it? How will you train them to grow even more in these three aspects of obedience?

4. Based on Ruth Bell Graham's comments, are you talking too much and not acting enough with your children, concerning obedience?

You might want to read the booklet, Under Loving Command, then discuss it together.

6
Dear Preacher,

"Parenting isn't the only influence on a child's development, but it's the one we can do the most about."

- Michael Popkin, author, teacher

As a pastor who has led numerous seminars on the art of parenting and purports to be some sort of child-rearing expert (I can see my wife smiling), I regularly field all kinds of questions on every conceivable parenting topic. You name it; I've been asked it.

I've been quizzed about everything from my personal perspective on potty training (something I had very little to do with, thanks, Nev.) to tips on launching grown children out into the world and all those burning questions in between.

But the questions I'm asked most often deal with the sometimes tricky, always challenging dynamics of disciplining, training and loving children. Here are seven of the most common ones, illustrated with a few comics from <u>Just a Simple Country Preacher</u> by Doug Marlette, a Thomas Nelson book that I have laughed with for years.

If I don't cover your question here, why not bring it up at your next small group meeting with a couple of other parents?

1. Can you share some specific things that hinder us from giving our children the time and attention that they need? I don't want to be blind to any normal activities that may be competing with my desire to spend time with my kids.

Often it's the normal, everyday "good" things we're involved in that actually may be at cross-purposes with our desire to be successful parents. For example, you may have great motives behind spending so many hours at work, but it can actually make you a stranger to your own family. Spending "me" time with our favorite hobbies – without ever including our children – can be a cause for resentment for them. Moms and dads need social activities, but an active social calendar is not our inherent right as adults. As parents we are called to multiply our lives <u>through</u>

our children, not apart from them.

God can probably point out several specific things we each can do as parents if we'll just stop and ask Him. For example, many of the activities on our "to do" lists — like exercise or running errands — can provide great opportunities for training our kids and can be lots of fun in the process. Why not spend some time thinking of creative ways to include your children in your day-to-day activities?

2. My kids (ages 4 and 2) frequently push and hit each other. Should I get involved in helping them solve their differences and or just let them *"work it out themselves?"*

Please do get involved. When young children "work it out themselves" without adult guidance, the result is usually not a just solution. The book of Proverbs says that foolishness — not wisdom — is "bound up in the heart of a child." That's where we come in as parents.

Obviously we cannot always be involved in every little disagreement between our kids, but pushing and hitting "cross the line." Little children need to be taught not to solve their differences through fighting. So if a fight breaks out, I would counsel you parents to always jump in and stop it and then correct your kids every time. Don't warn, don't nag, spank! If we are diligent, we can dramatically lower the amount of fighting that goes on in our homes.

Just the other day my freshman in high school came home and mentioned that a good friend of hers said to her that day, "Becky, you and your brother and sister don't seem to ever fight. Why is that? I wish we didn't fight so much in our family."

Becky said, "Well, that's just the way we were raised."

3. Our two-year-old gets lots of attention from everyone in the whole family – parents and siblings alike – but it never seems to be enough. He often resorts to destructive behavior when he wants more attention. What should we do?

I would suggest earnest prayer, especially if you discover that he's fascinated with matches! Seriously though, a two-year-old is pretty young to be self-entertained. At his age, he needs adult guidance in constructive ways to play. However, as he keeps growing, your goal should be to see that your son learns to play without always needing to be stimulated by others. As parents, we want all of our children to be learning self-control.

Work diligently towards this long-term goal. In the meantime, do not reward destructive behavior by giving him more attention. You don't want him to learn that he can get whatever he wants by pushing you until you give in. As parents, we need to be able to discern whether our children actually need attention or are just being selfish. If you know he is getting enough attention, be firm and don't yield. Ultimately, you want him to learn how to be content in his heart.

Like many other parenting issues, this requires a daily,

on-the-spot kind of wisdom. As parents, we get this kind of wisdom through the instruction and example of other parents, through God graciously giving us wisdom and, you guessed it, through personal experience in the good old school of life.

4. I'm divorced and when my kids come to visit me, they often complain about the kind of treatment they receive from my ex and from my ex's new mate. My kids say that they get yelled at, spanked and yanked around by the arm, etc. What should I do?

Unfortunately, this is a very "real life" kind of problem. There are no simple answers and I would need to know more details about your situation to give you a specific answer. (Usually there are some significant issues involved in this kind of situation than can't be shared publicly.)

In any event, encourage your children by making it clear to them that they are not personally at fault for any unreasonable action taken by a parent, step-parent or another adult. Our kids truly may have done something wrong, but that's no excuse for abuse. No matter what our children do, discipline and correction from us as parents needs to be patient, loving and just.

This is where a good church can be of great help to you. My wife and I would be happy to sit down and talk with you – with any of you readers, for that matter — about any parenting questions you have. Feel free to call us and maybe we can meet for coffee. After all, we're all in this together. As America's number one psychologist, Dr. James Dobson, has said, **"Parenting isn't for cowards."**

Occasionally we all might need specific help and ideas from others who are a little farther down the road in their parenting.

5. When it comes to disciplining our children, should we warn them first before we get around to spanking? And if so, how many times should we warn them before we spank them?

Every parent warns his or her children at times. But warning is a two-edged sword. Often the more times we warn a child before spanking him, the more he will delay obeying. Many children "learn" by a parent's behavior that they can wait until the third or fourth warning – or a warning that is delivered with loud threats – before taking mom or dad seriously.

Take it from me, you do not want to get involved in this kind of "bartering." Instead, first speak the child's name. Once your child answers "yes," then tell him or her what you expect. If your child goes against your word, please discipline him right then and there. We all know that discipline is "messy" and takes time, but believe me, the constant warning and nagging that can go on in our homes between parents and kids is much more wearing.

If you go right ahead and discipline your son or daughter immediately for bad behavior, your children soon

learn that they can't postpone obeying for two or three "warnings' worth." And when it comes to fighting between siblings, in our family we always try to spank the offender every time. No child ever needs a warning before being disciplined for that kind of behavior.

6. Sometimes I discipline my kids when I am angry. I yell at them and scold them and nag them. My parents did this all the time and I hate it. What can I do differently?

We have all smiled – and maybe cried a little, too – when we look in the mirror and recognize that we are a lot like our parents. Many of these similarities are inevitable, but some need to be avoided. Obviously it isn't good to yell at your kids. We may get angry when our kids break something in our homes, but we need to be able to control our anger.

What should you do when you feel yourself getting angry? First, take two or three deep breaths and try to get your emotions under control. Then follow through and correct your child. We have to be able to do both – both control our emotions and deliver the discipline. That's just part of the job description of being a good parent.

Remember, not all anger is bad. It can be a "right motivating" emotion for parents, if it is under control. Maybe that's what the Bible means when it tells us, "Be angry, but do not sin."

Another thing to consider is that you may not be correcting the problem soon enough. You may be letting something slide when it should be corrected – and since you let it go, the children continue their inappropriate behavior until you get angry. Try applying the discipline sooner, so that you correct the problem before you get so angry.

7. In thinking about the whole idea of being a successful parent, I realize that I do love my children very much and I really want to do what's right for them. But I'm having trouble "liking" the job of being a parent. Any ideas?

Welcome to the real world. Often there are parts of this job description that we don't like. But don't feel too guilty if you dislike certain aspects of being a parent; it doesn't mean you don't love your kids.

Being an adult means that we accept our responsibilities. And being a parent means that we accept the "whole enchilada." Our kids need our example of always being there for them – for the parts of parenting that we enjoy as well as the things that are frankly unpleasant. One wise man has calculated that "children are the sum of what their parents contribute to their lives." This is so true. Our children need us so, whether we feel like it or not.

Let me illustrate. Charles Francis Adams was a well-known political figure of the 19th century. He kept a diary, as did his son Brook. Both diaries are still in existence today, preserved as a timely testimony to the amazing influence we have in our children's lives – even when we're least aware of it.

Here is the father's entry for what he thought was just an ordinary day: "Went fishing with my son today – a day wasted."

The son's entry for that same day? "Went fishing with my dad today – it was the most wonderful day of my life!"

You just never know when you may be making a life-changing impact on your children. So take heart and stick it out, parent. Determine to remember the things that you enjoy about being a mother or father and make a concerted effort to delight in those things. As you deliberately highlight them and take energy from them, that energy can carry over into the areas of parenting that are more difficult for you. Remember how important the whole job is and how much it means – or will mean – to your children. Take pride in your position. After all, your work as a parent is extremely valuable. Don't let our culture draw you into elevating the value of "other things" over the enduring value of parenting well.

Stick with it parent. Don't believe the lie that states, "It is the quality of the time spent with your kids that counts, not the quantity." This is a lie. **Quantity is crucial!**

A final word of practical wisdom is in order here. Never let your kids know about the aspects of parenting that you don't like. They might take it too personally and then think that you don't like them. (Or maybe use it against you!)

Chapter 6 - Discussion Questions

1. Which of these seven questions do you identify with, the most?

2. What is another pressing question, that is on your mind, that you don't really have a good answer to?

3. Do you know one or two sets of wise parents that you can (and will) turn to in order to get advice on questions you may have?

4. What would make this kind of counsel easy? What would make this kind of counsel hard?

7
Frontline Families

"If your Christianity doesn't work at home, then it doesn't work at all. Therefore you must not try to export it."

- Howard Hendricks

Author's note: This chapter is a recap of a message I gave at our Annual Pastors' Conference a few years back, where our theme was "Building a Great Commission Family." We briefly traced our movement's shared beliefs on marriage and the family and attempted to provide a succinct, scriptural basis for those beliefs.

This chapter is kind of hard-nosed.

It is by no means a comprehensive theological treatment of these topics, some of which are frankly controversial both in our culture and in Christianity at large.

But I believe it provides crucial insights into the dynamic relationship between having a healthy Christian family and being committed to fulfilling the Great Commission. And I believe that this paper accurately reflects our association of churches' beliefs - concerning marriage and the family.

For over a quarter of a century, we have all been thankful to see how God has built and strengthened the many marriages and families in our association of churches. We have always felt that what God has taught us in the area of marriage and family was central to our understanding of God's will for our lives. Our shared beliefs on both marriage and children are one of our core values and have helped establish us as a movement.

I want to remind us of five standards that we have sought to follow in our families – specifically those standards that we have practiced and taught over the years that are critical to building truly healthy, outreach-minded, Christian families.

Looking back over the last 25 years, we are justifiably proud of how rare divorce is in our movement. In fact, it is hardly ever even spoken of. We are also very proud of the caliber of sons and daughters we are now raising up and have begun releasing into the world.

We find ourselves, as a movement of churches, involved in helping to rebuild hurting families throughout our cities and countries. My hope is that we will not only remember these core values that have securely established our own marriages and families and have "brought us safely thus far," but that we will also proclaim these distinctives to this very desperate and love-hungry world.

Following are five beliefs that have marked our movement as it relates to our understanding of the family and how we hold marriage in high regard in the church.

1. Our commitment to obeying the Great Commission within our families has safeguarded and strengthened our families in foundational ways.

We have understood that our marriages, children and home lives have served as a "base of operations" for reaching out with the Gospel. Just as a soldier who is active in fighting for God's Kingdom enjoys His special protection and blessing, so too our marriages have enjoyed His special protection and blessing.

We are probably not even fully aware of how our initial commitment to sharing the Gospel, and our continuing involvement in spreading the Gospel, have sanctified our home lives.

"There is one who scatters, yet increases all the more, And there is one who withholds what is justly due, but it results only in want. The generous man will be prosperous, and he who waters will himself be watered."

- Proverbs 11:24, 25

"A Christian marriage... serves a threefold purpose: to enrich the lives of the man and woman, to create a family, and to further the kingdom of God."

- Jack Roeda

Since our earliest day, we who are married have sought to obey the spirit of Paul's encouragement when he wrote to the Corinthians who were married to live "as though they were not." Marriage has always been held in honor among us, but it has never been allowed to serve as an excuse for not being involved in this great struggle of reaching our world for Christ.

Sadly, almost every Christian book that has been written on the family during the last two decades has ignored this commitment to sharing the Gospel. But we believe that this commitment is absolutely foundational to a healthy Christian marriage and family. We have practiced, modeled and taught that we – as *families* – need to be devoted to reaching out with the Good News if our families ever hope to be biblically sound.

While we have highly valued the importance of the Great Commission as a salting and energizing influence in our home lives, we recognize that we still have a lot to learn. The Scripture sets the bar very high:

"He who loves father or mother more than Me is not worthy of Me; and he who loves son or daughter more than Me is not worthy of Me."

- Matthew 10:37

2. When we speak of a man's family being devoted to the Great Commission, we are talking about active service and labor, not simply passive church attendance.

By this we mean three things:

- That a man's wife and children serve alongside him as "fellow workers."

"But when Priscilla and Aquila heard him, they took him aside and explained to him the way of God more accurately."

- Acts 18:26

- That our wives are proud to be involved in this "noble struggle" and our children are proud to be vitally involved in serving.

"Let our sons in their youth be as grown-up plants, and our daughters as corner pillars fashioned as for a palace."

- Psalms 144:12

- That while it is good to attend church, it is even better for a Christian family to be involved in "laying down" their lives by serving the church and laboring in the Gospel.

"For whoever wishes to save his life shall lose it; but whoever loses his life for My sake and the gospel's shall save it."

- Mark 8:35

3. We are committed to men leading in their families and women submitting to their husband's leadership.

"Wives, be subject to your own husbands, as to the Lord. For the husband is the head of the wife, as Christ also is the head of the church, He Himself being the Savior of the body. But as the church is subject to Christ, so also the wives ought to be to their husbands in everything. Husbands, love your wives, just as Christ also loved the church and gave Himself up for her; that He might sanctify her ... "

- Eph. 5:22-26

"If Christ's love for the Church is to be the model for marriage, then this much both partners can learn: You have to put up with a lot, and you have to cherish a lot."

- George McCauley

While this commitment to differing roles for men and women is not currently popular in our culture, it is a central tenet in our understanding of Christian marriage. This core belief continues to dismay our society. The world does not understand that both men and women have equal standing in the eyes of the Lord, yet different roles.

We will, however, continue to teach this vital truth for the sake of order in our homes and to model two godly qualities – Christian servant leadership and Christian submission – to a lost and needy world.

"The problems of America are the problems our families are facing – multiplied a million-fold."

- Dwight D. Eisenhower

Even pagan, ancient Rome recognized that men need to lead out in their families. Yet they crumbled as a society when they gave up on this family order.

"The most important feature of those families was the authority of the father. It would be difficult to overestimate the influence they had upon the history and destiny of Rome, but... the stern face of the traditional father had faded out by the second century A.D. Instead we see on every hand the flabby face of the son of the house, the eternal spoiled child

of society, who has grown accustomed to luxury and lost all sense of discipline ... also many women evaded the duty of maternity for fear of losing their looks and many were not content to live their lives by their husband's side."

- Daily Life in Ancient Rome

4. When we evaluate a man for leadership, we look first at the soundness of his marriage and family before evaluating his ministry skills or other credentials.

"It is a trustworthy statement: if any man aspires to the office of overseer, it is a fine work he desires to do. An overseer, then, must be above reproach, the husband of one wife, temperate, prudent, respectable, hospitable, able to teach, not addicted to wine or pugnacious, but gentle, uncontentious, free from the love of money. He must be one who manages his own household well, keeping his children under control with all dignity (but if a man does not know how to manage his own household, how will he take care of the church of God?); and not a new convert, lest he become conceited and fall into the condemnation incurred by the devil. And he must have a good reputation with those outside the church, so that he may not fall into reproach and the snare of the devil."

- 1 Timothy 3:1-7 (NAS)

"He must manage his own family well, with children who respect and obey him."

- 1 Timothy 3:4 (NLT)

"For this reason I left you in Crete, that you might set in order what remains, and appoint elders in every city as I directed you, namely, if any man be above reproach, <u>the husband of one wife, having children who believe, not accused of dissipation or rebellion. For the overseer must be above reproach as God's steward</u>, not self-willed, not quick-tempered, not addicted to wine, not pugnacious, not fond of sordid gain, but hospitable, loving what is good, sensible, just, devout, self-controlled, holding fast the faithful word which is in accordance with the teaching, that he may be able both to exhort in sound doctrine and to refute those who contradict."

- Titus 1:5-9 (NAS)

"<u>An elder must be well thought of for his good life. He must be faithful to his wife, and his children must be believers who are not wild or rebellious. An elder must live a blameless life because he is God's minister.</u>"

- Titus 1:6-7a (NLT)

Since Scripture tells us that a man's family is the central proving ground where his heart and leadership ability is revealed, we have always started here. In Timothy and Titus, much is made of a man's ability in his home.

The main thing is to be humble and accountable – to a good friend, to a fellow husband or father, to your small group leader, to your pastor, etc. This is not easy. It seems that we are more open to receiving help in any other arena of ministry; but with our families it can be a very touchy thing.

However, if we are humble, God will bless us.

There comes a time when our children become adults and will

give an account for their own lives. But it is obvious that while our children are still at home, we have a great responsibility to be good managers, good parents and leaders and spiritual guides to our children. We are responsible.

"How can a man be a believer in Jesus Christ, and yet have a cold and hard heart in the things of the Kingdom toward his children and mate? You will find that where sons and daughters have turned out a curse to their parents, and those parents have been Christians, it might have been attributed by this – that while the parents have been Christians, they were not Christians at home."

"I believe nine out of ten such cases can be explained that way."

- Charles Spurgeon

"A man ought to live so that everybody knows he is a Christian... and most of all, his family ought to know."

- D. L. Moody

"The family and the home can never exert their proper influence on our world, while ignoring the Bible's exhortation calling for discipline and a recognition of authority. If children do not learn this at home, they will go out into society without a proper attitude toward authority and law. There is always the exceptional child, but the average tells us that children are largely what the home has made of them."

- Billy Graham

**5. Because a man's "credentials" rest in his family, we have
never asked a man to sacrifice his family for the sake of his
ministry.**

*"Marriage is a testing ground for one's integrity, courage
and character."*

- J. Allen Petersen

It is hard to imagine any one of us leading God's people if we
have lost their respect in any area. And in this arena of the family,
the respect of our congregations is vital.

Our world is still looking to the church for answers to the
challenges we all face in marriage and with our children. We have
always sought to model the truth we preach within our own families.
If we lose this position of respect, we have lost all hope of genuinely
moving our audience to embrace God's truth concerning marriage
and the family.

Regardless of a man's gift or abilities, when there are needs in
his home, he must make it his priority to apply himself to those
needs first.

*"A church within a church, a republic within a republic, a
world within a world, it is spelled in four letters – HOME. If
things go right there, they go right everywhere. The front door
of the home is the foundation of the Church, as well as the
State."*

- Thomas DeWitt Talmage

"And this I say for your own benefit; not to put a restraint upon you, but to promote what is seemly, and to secure undistracted devotion to the Lord."

- 1 Cor. 7:35

There is a tension point here. We believe that a life – with marriage and family – lived in sacrifice for our Lord is pleasing to Him. But we also know that at times a man needs to concentrate his focus more on building up his family.

We have encouraged this in our movement of churches – not as an allowance for the flesh, but as a very real responsibility that at times needs to be addressed.

Our goal in this is to see our marriages and families built up in such a way that we can then all together, as husband and wife, as parents and children, resume a life of sacrifice to advance the kingdom of God.

For further study:

To find out more about our movement, our association of churches, and our shared vision and core values, I would suggest you visit the Great Commission Association of Churches web site. www.gcachurches.org

Chapter 7 – Discussion Questions:

1. Has your marriage and family so far been a *"base of operations"* for the Gospel?

2. Are your wife and children "fellow workers" with you? Is there some ministry or outreach you can do as a couple and a family?

3. Are you and your wife in agreement on each of your roles? What is the greatest challenge for you in fulfilling your role?

4. Concerning your humility and accountability, have you recently asked someone you trust how you could improve in your parenting?

5. A tension point is described, living sacrificially for the Lord, yet caring for our families. Discuss this tension point with your spouse and with some other fathers, perhaps in your small group. What will help you to keep a proper balance?

8
Our Most Challenging Struggle

"There are few, if any, that would devote up to twenty years out of their prime-of-life, in hopes of saving and raising their children. But that was my principal intent, however unskillfully I may have managed it."

- Susanna Wesley

Twenty some odd years ago, when relatively few of us in our association of churches had children of school age, we had no collective experience in educating children at all. But we did have one thing going for us – a strong, motivating fear.

We did not want this world to capture our kids!

We were concerned about turning our young children over to the public school system and having them hear and observe all kinds of crazy behavior at such an impressionable age. So, with very little insight and encouragement from anyone, we took it upon ourselves to begin teaching our children. We focused on both the basics of reading, writing and arithmetic (something we thought we could do better than the public schools at that time) and the character that we felt needed to be built into our kids.

We weren't necessarily sure at the time what to do when they got past the 3 R's, but we believed that we could at least start them right.

Wanting to protect our children from the world is a righteous desire. But "the world" is only one of our problems. Often, it seems to me, we parents get all worked up in striving against just one of our spiritual opponents, when the Bible tells us that we have three – the world, the flesh and the devil. All three are out to derail our kids. All three have different methods to harm them. And all three need to be recognized as our enemies.

Our three enemies

If I concentrate on recognizing the false philosophies of this world, I do well. The world does have an arrogant, godless agenda. But if I think that all of my trials and my family's trials are caused by this world's system, I am naive. My flesh is also very active and the devil is continually lying to me.

If I think that the world is my only opponent, I can easily become an isolationist. The problem with running away from the world is that everywhere I go I still take my flesh with me – and padding after my flesh comes the devil.

If I work to overcome the desires of my flesh, I do well. My flesh is always trying to drag me down. I need discipline to train my kids to fight to overcome their flesh for the purpose of godliness. There is this constant struggle between my flesh and my new spirit. But the flesh is only one of my opponents; I still have two others. If I become too overly concerned with the flesh, I can easily become a legalist.

If I focus on resisting the schemes of the devil, I do well. The devil is always lying to me and trying to deceive me. But if I throw all of my effort into fighting him, I still have my old flesh to deal with, as well as the world. If I concentrate solely on the devil, I can easily become superstitious.

Obviously we need to be vigilant on all three fronts with all three opponents. We need to be circumspect, which means that we need to see in all directions. This is the hallmark of a vigilant Christian parent.

But about fifteen years into the process of preparing my kids for adulthood, I found myself not as concerned about the world or the devil as I once was. I'm not naïve. I know that we live in a hostile society.

But I am convinced that the worst enemy we face is our own flesh.

Public enemy #1

Laziness and a lack of sustained effort will trip up more of our youth in their education than any other foe. Our most serious challenge in educating our children comes from the flesh, both our flesh as the teacher and their flesh as the student. None of us are as disciplined as we need to be.

I believe that laziness and a lack of discipline in our homes is slowing down the development of our children more than any other thing. I don't think that we recognize this in our churches like we should. Home schooling requires more discipline and more structure then we may ever have first imagined.

(On a side note, I have always been a little leery of self-paced curricula, especially considering that most of the "selves" I have dealt with are inherently lazy and easily distracted.)

Why is it that almost every mom gets a little anxious about those end-of-the-year, national, academic tests, that happen every spring? Some are called Iowa Basic Skills Tests, some are called the California Achievement Tests. Both can inspire dread.

After all, haven't we all done a pretty good job in keeping the world outside our walls? The reason why we sweat a little is because we know that our daily home school habits and family discipline for the year are soon to be revealed.

"There are few, if any, that would devote up to twenty years out of their prime-of- life, in hopes of saving and raising their children. But that was my principal intent, however unskillfully I may have managed it."

- Susanna Wesley

We need to get more serious about this. Sarah Edwards and Susannah Wesley would be considered legalistic by most of us, but they won in the end with all of their children. We'll take a look at their lives and the fruit of their methods in their children's lives in a later chapter.

Good grades v. character

Now I don't believe that good grades are our only goal. We all have spoken to educated people who lack character. But if we really are winning in the development of godly character, why shouldn't our youth take this same godly character and shine in any high school in the country?

Our kids are each very different. They have all kinds of abilities and levels of aptitude. My own children come in many flavors. They may not all get an A, but they can all do well in school.

While some of my kids may not be as good at school work as some of their siblings, they still need to learn to work at it. We recognize that each one of them is shaped by God with specific talents and strengths. The trick is to identify that "talent" and develop it.

Some kids excel in music. Some excel in sports. But all of them need academics, if for no other reason than to show a future employer that they can stick with something and finish it. For this reason, they must win with the books. To succeed in their work in the future, they first need to have been trained in the "work" of school now.

Twenty years ago many of us thought that formal education was unnecessary. We were convinced that every male in our young Christian movement would be raised up as a full-time pastor from within the church in just a few years. After all, didn't God want every man to aspire to the noble work of pastoring? And didn't Jesus Himself train his followers – not through the rigors of intellectual book learning – but through a close, working relationship with Him that could only be classified as "on-the-job training?"

But that just didn't happen. Consequently, many dads needed to go back to school to gain the educational skills they needed to provide for their families.

I fully realize that college is not the only avenue to job skills. But most of us have been to college and although we haven't all used the training we received there, we are proud to have finished school and usually we want a similar experience for our own children. As one wise person has said, "A college education seldom hurts a man if he is willing to learn a little something after he graduates."

But no matter which path of further education our teens choose, hard work, self-discipline and mastery of the flesh are vital right here and now.

Don't get me wrong. I believe that we are raising some pretty good kids. For the most part, they seem to stack up well compared with other churches. At a recent teen conference, the camp director told me several times how exceptional the youth in our association of churches were – and he primarily deals with church youth camps all year long! (At one large YMCA campground here in Colorado, the worst group of kids they deal with every year comes from the largest and most well known church in the city!)

However, are our children as educated as they need to be? I'm not talking about raw brainpower here. I am not at all concerned with how smart they are or what their IQs are. The issue is, are they disciplined in their studies? Real intelligence comes from applied effort. God help us if our children are good kids but are not prepared for real life and have not applied themselves. Our youth simply cannot afford to spend a lot of time (and money) *"finding themselves."*

Musings about home school

I have often wondered whether home schooling is really the best option for everyone – especially if we are not able to bring a clear structure and pattern to our home classrooms and if we are not as firm as we need to be.

I am well aware of the serious discipline problems that occur at times in many public, private and charter school classes. And I recognize that some classes, because of weaknesses in the teacher, wind up a total waste. But there is an education to be found there, in every one of our high schools, if our kids work for it. And I have yet to see a home-educator provide a high school education that equals the academics required for one of our kids to compete against 200 other classmates and still pull down an "A."

We need to be careful of over-praising our kids when their accomplishments are gained within the rather limited arena of our own homes or churches. We all want to encourage our youth with our support, no matter how simple the achievement might be, but have they really accomplished something?

It's a big world out there, but our kids can win out in the world if we prepare them. They can shine in every way, even when competing with the crude and the secular and the lost.

What about the drinking and the drugs, you say? What about the immorality in the public school system? What about the slouching, arrogant attitude found in almost every high school in every state?

Well, what about it? If our youth are so weak that they wind up running with the wrong crowd, then we know where the problem lies.

And the problem is not *"those other kids."* It never is. The problem is in how we train them.

Let me illustrate how our kids can successfully demonstrate strength of character no matter what the "other kids" are doing:

I remember when we first let our oldest boy Josh begin attending public school. He started in 8ᵗʰ grade, the last year of junior high school. We had registered him earlier, so I drove him up to the school, told him to go through the front doors, turn right and introduce himself to the secretary there in the office. They would take it from there.

When he got off the bus that night, he came in the front door, sat down at our dining room table and immediately told us a pretty wild story. His little sisters were all eyes and ears. (None of them had gone to public school yet.)

Anyway, he introduced himself to the principal, who told Josh to follow him down the hall. They got around the first corner and saw a circle of kids. They were surrounding another student who was lying on his side on the floor, all doubled up.

"What's wrong? What's the matter, Steve?" the principal asked him.

"Susie kicked me in the nuts!" the injured boy squawked. (At this point, all of my little girls' mouths flew open.)

"Well, you're not dead," the principal said. "Get up and go to class. The show's over! Everyone get to class. Josh, follow me."

So he did.

And in his first class, Josh ran into a bully.

The kid said, "Who are you?"

"I'm Josh," my son replied.

Then the boy asked, "Where did you move in from?"

Josh said, "Well, I didn't move in from anywhere. I was home schooled."

"Home schooled!" the boy retorted. "Are you a home boy? Then I think I'll call you Homer."

The bully kept riding my son throughout the day.

I didn't really know what to say to Josh. Obviously I hadn't prepared him for some old-fashioned fist fighting, which at that moment I felt might be the best solution. I was sort of ticked off.

But I forgot about the incident, great dad that I am. Josh continued going to school and I just forgot to ask him about this little bully.

A couple weeks went by and I remembered.

"How's it going with that boy who's been riding you, Josh?" I asked.

"I took care of it, Dad," Josh answered. "We had phys ed and it was dodge ball."

My first thought was, "Great! Josh probably plastered that bully."

But that wasn't what happened at all.

It seems that the coach asked Josh to be a captain and

pick his team. Now Josh had been reading in Proverbs about blessing your enemies and had been thinking about how he could befriend this boy. So, responding to the Spirit, Josh picked this boy first to be on his team.

I would have never thought of that. But God thought of that and impressed it on my boy's heart. Josh had been praying about it. And the boys became friends!

No matter what age our children are, they can stand up and trust in God right alongside us. God will help them and speak to them and give them specific direction just like He does for us.

The problem is not certain teachers, certain classes or certain high schools. We need to be careful about blaming others for our kids' condition. It seems to me that most – if not all – of the difficulties that Neva and I have had in raising our children are self-inflicted. We need to stop blaming others and stop being afraid of the world. Often we just whine about the world and make excuses. *Well, parent, we will never win if all we do is whine!*

Instead we need to get serious about training our youth to exhibit a stronger, internal, self-restrained, personal discipline. The principle "others may, but I cannot" needs to be understood by and applied in the heart of each of our teens. Others may do something, but we will not. Others may jump off a cliff, but we will not. And there is good reason why we will not. We are trying to win them to Christ, remember?

Do we have dreams for our teens – or do we just want them to avoid getting into trouble? If we have dreams for them, then we must do our part to see that they are prepared for life so that those dreams can become reality.

Here are two specific lists that I use all the time in our weekend parenting seminars that I hope you'll find helpful. By the time our kids reach age 12, they need to have the character traits in the first list (The Measure of a Boy or Girl) under their belts – or at least be making good progress in those areas. By the time they graduate from high school and are getting ready to move out into the world, they need to have learned, grown in and shown appreciation for the traits in the second list (The Measure of a Teen). You'll find both lists repeated in the appendix, with Bible verses to encourage each trait.

I hope they will not only encourage you by how far your kids have come in their character development, but also will help you gauge in a very practical way the work you still have to do to ready them for the time when you'll set them loose!

The Measure of a Boy/Girl
1. Obedient
2. Pays attention
3. Learns to share, is considerate of others
4. Accepts discipline without anger or pouting
5. Responds to direction to control emotions
6. Starts building a reputation
7. Starts developing good work habits
8. Can handle pain

The Measure of a Teen
1. Has a sense of purpose
2. Has good work habits (Is a self-starter)
3. Distinguishes himself by good deeds
4. Is strong against peer pressure
5. Develops the right friends
6. Is not naive
7. Values parent's instruction in his heart
8. Trusts in God's Word

9. Manages his emotions
10. Has good speech
11. Not foolish, is sensible
12. Has a good countenance
13. Respects others, protects siblings
14. Honors women
15. Knows how to handle suffering
16. Is trustworthy and faithful
17. Has biblical understanding of grace and forgiveness

"He will turn the hearts of the fathers to their children, and the hearts of the children to their fathers; or else I will come and strike the land with a curse."

- Malachi 4:6

Anyway, the reason I wanted to share these points on what we are trying to instill into our kids, is because I keenly want us <u>all</u> to win as parents. *Every one of us!*

And to have a clear focus and goals for our kids.

I deeply desire that every family in each of our churches has this chance.

To repeat, I am convinced that - *We will never win if all we ever do as parents is complain about this crazy world.* Do we catch ourselves habitually whining about this world, our flesh, and the devil and just make excuses, and not really bear down on ourselves and on our children as we must?

My prayer is that we will be strong and bear down when we need to.

Chapter 8 – Discussion Questions

1. Of our three enemies - the world, the flesh, and the devil - is there one you have overemphasized to the neglect of the other two?

2. How do you react to the statement in this chapter, *"I believe that laziness and a lack of discipline in our home is slowing down the development of our children more than any other thing"*?

3. Are you setting an example in your own life for your children, in striving against laziness and lack of discipline?

4. What steps will you take to help your children make progress in this area?

9
More Discipline, More Instruction and Much More Affection

"Affection is responsible for nine-tenths of whatever solid and durable happiness there is in our lives."

- C.S. Lewis (from The Four Loves)

As I think about how to truly encourage you dads who are dead serious about winning with your kids, my thoughts turn toward our sons and daughters. So what's on my mind? Three things: discipline, instruction and affection.

But before I write another word, I will start with an admission. I admit that I am not a theologian. (Stop laughing.) If I were to write several pages on a particular theological position, most of you who know me would either smile wryly or feign attention out of politeness. But either way, I would not be taken seriously – and rightly so, for I am no theologian. In that arena, I know not whereof I speak.

But when it comes to raising kids, I know what I'm talking about, guys.

Ever notice how our media sarcastically accuses Christians of being narrow-minded individuals who like our answers delivered in small, simple doses? Although years ago we bridled at their condescending attitudes, I think their accusations have truly affected our thinking today. In a kind of pendulum swing, we now often resist instruction that is short and simple.

Here in America we live in a society that is hyper-introspective, self-absorbed and glorifies the individual. By and large, Christianity has gone along with this. However, as we look for answers from this isolated perspective, we tend to accept only those answers that are specifically tailored to our individual circumstances. Any solution that is more general in nature we tend to look down on.

It seems that we have unconsciously agreed that everyone is so unique that it is almost impossible to bring wisdom from one person's experience to bear on another person's life and family. We can easily become convinced that the solutions we need can never be found in our neighbor's life and family experiences.

However, in reading the Bible for over 30 years, I haven't noticed much language that elevates individual wants or desires. What I *have* noticed is, in book after book, God speaks to all mankind with general, simple instructions that He wants (and expects) everyone to embrace.

Why? Because His answers work for all of us, not just for some of us! I only wish more of us would believe deep down in our hearts that His answers on parenting – though simple and general in nature – truly work if applied!

That said, after talking to literally hundreds of couples in the last few months, I am more convinced than ever that the answers to the main issues of parenting are simple and transferable. Therefore I will repeat my main premise yet again. One of the main things all moms and all dads need to recognize is that *our kids need more discipline, more instruction and much more affection – more than we ever imagined!*

Almost all of the instruction that I offer parents in my parenting seminar fits into one of these three categories.

However, before we delve into those three areas, let's take a look at a real life example of the benefits of applying general truths to individual circumstances.

A lesson from lambs

As a lot of you know, in the summer my kids enjoy raising market lambs and competing at our county fair. It is a hobby that I enjoy a lot and that the kids take pride in. I buy lambs once in awhile from a neighbor, often "left-over" lambs. If I buy a lamb at a sale, it is never one of the top five or ten lambs, but always a cheaper lamb down the line. I do raise a few lambs every year and sometimes I get a late lamb from one of my brothers' flocks. But I never start out with the best from other flocks.

Yet every summer, year after year, we Whitneys win an unfair share of classes and championships at the county fair when we show our lambs up against 200 other lambs from across the county.

We don't always start off with the best genetics. (In fact, oftentimes I deliberately buy a more average lamb – knowing that an even better lamb from that same farm has been sold and will show up at the county fair – just to see how I do.) But we beat them year after year. We have more trophies, belt buckles and ribbons than we know what to do with. Why?

Because the secret is in how you raise them! We apply the right technique with all of our show string and it never fails to turn out the right results. If we can do that with dumb sheep, imagine what we can do with children who are made in the image of God!

(Obviously, I am trying to take away any objections you might have before I get into my three concerns. And since you are all adults, you know what I am trying to do anyway. So please be patient with me. ☺)

A lesson from wrestling

Here's another example. A few days ago, my son Michael and I were watching a video on the spirit and drive that Dan Gable brought to coaching wrestling. In that short video, a fellow coach (who had won a number of NCAA championships himself) said with respect and honor, "When Dan Gable lays his hands on you, you are touched by grace."

He wasn't talking about Dan Gable's faith or spiritual lifestyle. That fellow coach was only trying to state the obvious: that when it came to instructing wrestlers on how to train and compete, Dan Gable knew what he was talking about.

Why did Gable have such an incredible string of championships at the University of Iowa in the 80's and early 90's? If you followed Iowa wrestling, you knew that he did not always get the best high school wrestlers. He got his share, but many incredible high school champions went to any one of over 20 other excellent programs across the country. However, Gable got more out of his kids year in and year out – because he knew what he was talking about.

We have to believe that our families are not so highly individualized or unique that we cannot take simple biblical principles, apply them and then see genuine change and real progress. We have to believe that the relationship issues and problems that come up in our families are not beyond solution, and that the solution may often be simple, general and supplied by someone outside the situation.

In short, we have to believe that we can learn vital, life-changing truths from each other!

Have you ever laughed (hopefully just inwardly) at the mom who says she has tried spanking her little two-year-old, but it didn't work? We all know that it does work. Well, I'm here to say that discipline, instruction and affection work, too. And not just for younger children. Once our kids hit the teen years, they need even bigger and bigger helpings of these three basic ingredients.

I'm just a fellow dad, but everywhere I go, I see these three needs over and over.

So trust me in this: *we need more discipline, more instruction and more affection in our parenting!*

The dynamics of discipline

First, let's talk about discipline. What do I mean by discipline? "No!" is what I mean. There is power, wisdom and strength in saying "No." The Bible is filled with the concept of "No." Eight of the Ten Commandments are "No." The "do not" instructions are general, simple and easily understood, and God gives them to us in big doses, page after page. From the first chapter to the last, God's Word is filled with all kinds of "No's." God is simple, strong and repetitive in teaching us over and over what not to do. Often it can seem that the "No's" of the Bible are just not that helpful anymore. However, if we think this, we are in error. The first things we teach our children always involve the concept of "No," and I dare say that much of our work as they get older still involves the discipline of saying "No" in one way or another.

Have you ever wondered whether too many "No's" will hurt your child's self-image? God doesn't seem to worry about it.

(Why are we so overly concerned about a healthy self-image anyway? Our prisons are filled with men who have strong self-images. Here in Colorado, a university study concluded that some of the strongest self-image scores in our state were found among the general prison population at Canyon City State Penitentiary.)

"There are times when parenthood seems nothing more than feeding the mouth that bites you."

- Peter De Vries

God knows that true and healthy confidence comes from obedience. When we disregard the "No's" in life, that is when we get hurt. It is our rebellion against rule and law that damages us. Brothers, we need more discipline and more obedience from our teens. To see this happen, we need to "lower the boom" over and over. We cannot "spare for their crying," whether they are three or 13. We generally should not yield to them or to their wants. As many of us know from our own personal experiences as teenagers (yes, we were all young once, too!), many of the wants of youth will often only dissipate our kids' effectiveness in life. The word "No" is a good word. There is nothing wrong or old-fashioned about "No."

One of the biggest "No's" that we as parents will be tested in with our teens is whether we will release them to their peers when we should not. I don't know how many times I have talked to parents who somehow wish they could draw their kids back from their peer relationships, but are now at their wits' end as to how to do it.

It would have been better if they had never let them loose so quickly in the first place. If our sons and daughters are ever more loyal to their friends than to their parents and siblings, then we need to change things, yesterday if possible. It is critical that we reclaim our teens' loyalties, no matter what the cost, even when it seems too late. We must recapture their hearts.

I saw a program on ABC's Primetime called "Whatever It Takes – A Child's Last Chance." In this piece, the reporter was talking to parents who were taking radical steps to recapture their teenage children. The reporter asked each of six sets of parents the same question: "Is it worth having your son hate you to see the change he needs?" All six couples simply answered, "Yes!"

If you know me, you know I do not believe in running away from the world. On the contrary, I believe in letting our kids go out and impact this world for Christ. My kids have been doing this in high school as well as in college. We are not afraid of this world, nor should our kids ever pick up any kind of fear from any one of us parents concerning this world. After all, "greater is He who is in you, than he who is in the world."

But if they are our kids, then we need to ask ourselves whether they are still ours – or whether they are really "owned" by others?

When it comes to the discipline I am applying in my relationship with my children, my personal evaluation questions are:

- Do my standards of discipline impress both fellow believers and the people of this world that I am attempting to reach?
- Is my discipline healthy, right, filled with common sense and attractive to the lost?

This doesn't mean that the world will agree with my methods. But the question is, do they want what I have? Does the discipline that I seek to instill in my kids lead to accomplishments and are those accomplishments attractive for the gospel?

Instruction on instruction

Second, our kids need more instruction.

Please don't say to yourself, "But they know the answer.

There's no need to repeat it. They already know what I am trying to tell them."

They don't know it, if they don't do it!

If they aren't practicing what you are talking about, as a part of their habits in life, they really don't "know" the instruction. It is not yet part of their makeup.

If you told your neighbor something and he said, "I know that already" – but hadn't shown any fruit in that area – you wouldn't necessarily believe that he really knew what you were talking about. You would keep trying to gently instruct him as long as he would listen. Usually with a neighbor we lose our audience after a while, but if he kept coming back for instruction, we would keep speaking. We would speak as winsomely as possible, but we would keep speaking.

With our children we have the opportunity to keep speaking. I encourage all of us to keep instructing, teaching, speaking, reading to and helping them until we see the fruit we are looking for. Our kids don't really have it until they speak it, until it is on their lips.

If they aren't patient, they aren't patient – and they don't really know what the Bible has to say about the subject. If they can't put on a Christ-like countenance and smile, they really don't know what the Bible has to say about being filled with the Spirit. We need to keep instructing and setting the example until we see the right results.

We need to keep instructing them in the simple, little things as well as in the bigger issues. Most of our instruction will be on the little things. Life is made up of hundreds and thousands of little things. I was blessed a while back by fellow dad Mark Darling making "a mountain out of a molehill" in instructing his boy to iron his pants. It was probably unpleasant. It probably involved a confrontation. It could have seemed petty, to both Mark and his son. But Mark kept instructing.

Instructing is not just talk. It involves consistent follow-through in every situation, hour by hour, day by day. We can't just throw it out there and then say to ourselves, "Well, at least I told them what to do." That's not enough, folks. *We need to tell them what to do until they do it!*

We cannot rest or quit until they receive our instruction. By receive, I mean to accept it into their hearts and incorporate it into their actions. I am not talking about nagging here. But if we ask them to clean up their rooms, they have to clean up their rooms.

In most instruction there is usually some element of discipline woven in, but that's okay. Keep instructing them and telling them what to do and what not to do, over and over, until they do it on their own.

Again my bottom line in evaluating my instruction is: Is it winsome for the gospel and a good example to the lost? Do the lost want what I have – or at least the fruit of it?

As the Bible says, "The ways of the Lord are right." Even neighbors or family members who are not yet believers often appreciate God's truth and its results at this most basic level.

Much more affection

Lastly, we need more affection.

After reading my thoughts on discipline and instruction, do you think that I'm too heavy-handed and serious to appreciate and enjoy affection? That I just threw this last section in for good measure?

Nothing could be farther from the truth. We do show affection in our family, every day with every child. We don't want our sons and daughters to begin to grow apart from our affection. Dennis Clark, a fellow dad and good friend, has offered this simple but effective advice, "Every day, a look, a word, a touch."

We have practiced this kind of affection for decades. Just as we naturally hugged them when they were two years old, we need to hug them and tickle and squeeze them and wrap our arms around them when they are twelve and sixteen and twenty-two. Although I am reserved in public, believe me: we are very affectionate in our home. It's a shame when parents are physically estranged from sons and daughters and the children estranged from us. Moms need to keep hugging sons and daughters and so do fathers.

Once again our society has a hard time understanding how we can balance discipline and instruction with affection. So they go to extremes to caricaturize Christian men as either stern, black-robed prophets or soft, easy-going pushovers.

However, God demands that fathers be both firm and loving. Our families need it. Strong at times, as well as fun loving. Serious, as well as playful. Able to "read them the riot act" and then kiss them good night.

Many parents are not affectionate enough. It is ironic that if we do not show sufficient affection when we should, we often overcompensate and wind up being too permissive later on.

The wise dad prays for his child's heart. But the even wiser dad prays for it, and then reaches out and grabs it!

Make no mistake. Our affection as parents will be very attractive to the lost. They will be drawn to our methods as well as our fruit. If we want to impact this world, then we need to bring the world into our homes and show them our affection.

The warmth in my family has won more hearts than anything I have ever said or done. It is very, very attractive to this dying world.

In summary, almost every week I talk with parents who are struggling. My first prayer is that they'll have heart enough to receive what I am saying and then to act on it. Because I know that these three things work–discipline, instruction and affection–

I am confident that if they humble themselves before the Lord and do exactly what God shows them, they will succeed.

"Train up a child in the way he should go, Even when he is old he will not depart from it."

- Proverbs 22:6

Chapter 9 – Discussion Questions

1. One of the biggest areas we will need to say "no" to our kids, is in not releasing them to their peers. Are your children more loyal to their friends than they are to you? In other words, do their friends *"own them"*?

2. If so, what will you do to recapture their hearts?

3. In what specific instructions to your kids do you tire the easiest and want to quit?

4. What is your view toward affection? Good? Important? Unnecessary?

5. Does affection come easily or hard for you in regards to your children? Toward your spouse? How can you improve toward both?

10
How Confident are You?

"The thing that impresses me most about America is the way parents obey their children."

- The Duke of Windsor

I talk to many pastors in our association of churches in the course of a month, so I get to hear a lot of dedicated guys talk about their home lives. In every case, I'm proud to say, our families are our first priority.

They are – rightly so – more important than our ministries or our work. Not one of us is content with progress at the office or in our churches, if the result is setbacks at home. We know that any victories won outside the home ring hollow if we are not winning with our children.

During the grade school years we can be pretty confident about our children. We know that we can mold their characters and instill good habits. We have seen it patterned by others and have experienced the blessing of following the book of Proverbs personally. Even when we get frustrated with our younger kids, we know what the best "medicine" is – love and faithfulness and discipline on our part.

Fellow dad Tom Dunham put it best when he said, "There are no strong-willed children – just weak-willed parents."

So when things get ragged in our families, I firmly believe that our main need is to strengthen our resolve as parents. This is the cure for families in our neighborhoods and for the many new families in our churches as well.

When a young couple comes to me feeling overwhelmed – and tells me that they have attempted to apply the book of Proverbs at home, but to no avail – I can't help but smile inwardly. I know that the Scriptures *are* effective and that the book of Proverbs works without exception. This young couple just hasn't applied these principles correctly yet. But they can learn to apply them, and apply them with great success.

"Any parent . . . who has come to terms with God's claim of authority on his life needs little more to qualify as an effective parent."

-Earl Jabay

As committed Christians, most of us already have established a good foundation of love and affection in our families. But we frequently lack resolve. As parents, we desperately need resolve to add a supporting layer of strength and discipline to this platform of love and affection. In general, firmness and guidance are the top needs in our families.

Especially as our children get older.

As I said earlier, I'm confident that those of us with kids age

10 and under can get the job done. My concern is that as our children move beyond 10, it often seems that we parents begin to doubt ourselves. I know I can doubt myself. How can we be confident that we can shape the character of our 5-year-old for good – and yet be frustrated and insecure, feeling somehow that we do not have the same God-given power to shape the character of our 15-year-old for good?

All of us love our children unconditionally. We are generally very proud of them. But they can also shame us. We frequently see these two dynamics at work between a parent and young child at the supermarket. The kid may be an embarrassment, but we also know that deep down, Mom or Dad would die for that child.

It is a sad state of affairs when a young couple cannot invite someone over for dinner for fear of how three-year-old Johnny will act. But it is even worse to be the parents of that selfsame Johnny, who's now 13 years old, and *still* be afraid of how he will act.

By the time our kids are teens, we must be convinced in our hearts that they can discern good from evil and act appropriately. That they will not jump off a cliff just because their peers do. That they have a strong internal braking system. If we aren't sure, then we had better roll up our sleeves and get serious, because very soon our teens will be out on their own.

When my kids were young, I protected them from poor examples. Now that they're older, I expect them to *be* examples. And not just in church, but out in the real world, on their sports teams and in school.

Brothers, are we confident that we are really turning out a quality product?

I'm not talking about whether we believe in our kids. Of course we do. I'm talking about taking an honest, unbiased look at three

Here are a few questions to get the wheels turning:

- Are you as confident now that your teens will turn out right as you were when they were very young?
- Are you concerned about attitude problems or disrespectful speech in your teens, or do you just chalk it up to their age?
- Do you sometimes wonder if you're "losing" them?

We all smile when a group of six-year-olds sings in front of the whole church. We don't care if they hit the notes or not. But it's an entirely different matter when it's a group of 16-year-olds. At that age, simply trying is not good enough. Our kids need to be able to compete in this world and win.

There are many voices in our culture telling us that competition is bad. I maintain, however, that competition is life. There's just no getting around it. We all must compete in some way or another to function in this world. There is a lot of good, healthy self-identity found in a difficult job well done. Are our kids learning the lessons that hard work and the sharpening effect of a talented competitor can teach?

> *"The best security I can give my children is an unquenchable thirst for hard work. Neither intelligence nor talent is as valuable as the knack for hard work. Give your child this knack."*
>
> - Anonymous

A big part of our job as parents is to affirm our kids. We need to affirm and affirm and affirm some more. But we also need to evaluate and judge. Do our teens – especially our sons – know that the path to success is through hard work?

Talent is not the main ingredient in success. Talent is

everywhere in this world. Hard workers, however, are rare. Charm and a smile are easily learned and used, yet they will not pass as real currency in this world. Hard work will. Your son may be the apple of your eye, but does he know how to keep his nose to the grindstone? Has he learned how to compete, persevere and win through hard work?

Have you ever wondered whether, as a whole, our daughters are turning out better than our sons? If you have chosen to school your children at home, you may have noticed that unique issues arise for the home-schooled male when he hits his teenage years.

Our daughters generally view the home front as the central focus of their future lives; they can learn a lot of important things as they watch Mom function in the home as a live-in role model. *But what about our sons?* Our boys need to get out there and compete and win, for it is in the hunt that they will find themselves.

If our kids are 13 or 14 and we're concerned that they might not be winning in certain areas, then we'd better take up the slack and begin applying ourselves more diligently as parents. Pretty soon they'll be 18 and they'll be looking outside of our homes for their career training.

It is truly amazing. You love them every day – day after day – for 18 long years, and then suddenly one day they aren't there at the supper table. And you know that they will never be at the supper table again in quite the same way.

Get ready, folks.

"Children make parents grow up a lot more than parents make children grow up. You're going to be with your spouse throughout life, but your child is going to walk away from you. In one respect this requires more generosity – to dedicate yourself to someone who will walk away."
- James T. Burchnell

It's absolutely crucial to use the high school years to give our kids the chance to compete outside the home while they're still living in it. Sure, they will struggle at times and even fail occasionally. As they try their wings and experience the inevitable setbacks, they can come home, dialogue candidly about what's happening and get out there and try again. Each step of progress will increase their inner confidence that they have what it takes to make it in the real world.

Even if we don't utilize the public high schools, we must give our kids significant opportunities to compete, learn and grow outside of our homes and churches. Whether our teens opt for sports, music, clubs or whatever, each of them must be able to run his or her own race with confidence.

We cannot be afraid for them. If we are, then we need to honestly assess *why* we have cause for fear. If it's due to lack of character in a particular area, then we need to focus on equipping them in that area until we're sure they can get out there and win in life.

We have to be convinced that they can say "No!" to the pressures of this world, that they are strong enough inside not to whine about how "all their friends are doing it." We have to be sure that they have dealt with their own tendency to be lazy and have persisted in working hard until they have truly seen the value of labor.

"Manual labor to my father was not only good and decent for its own sake but, as he was given to saying, 'It straightens out one's thoughts.'"

- Mary Ellen Chase

The school of life

Those who choose home schooling in the early grades can often do much better in preparing their children academically than the public schools can. The public schools just cannot compete with the level of individual instruction a child receives in a home school setting. But let's not kid ourselves about our ability to give them a well-rounded education as they get older. Can we actually teach honors calculus, biochemistry, biology and physiology as well as the professionals in our public high schools? Even if we can, why wouldn't we want our children to compete and excel in those same high schools, all the while having their senses being actively trained to discern good and evil?

Neva and I chose to home school our children when they were younger. We had just a few specific reasons. We wanted to make sure that we had them at home for a few more years, especially during those early, formative years when kids so easily pick up bad habits from others. And we thought we could do a pretty good job of teaching the three R's.

But, realistically, home schooling our kids all the way through high school just isn't the ultimate solution many of us once thought it was. In fact, I am convinced that much plain old selfishness runs under the home school flag. By that I mean, too many committed Christians are hiding out from their God-given responsibilities to make an impact in this world, all under the self-righteous banner of home schooling to "protect" their children.

I don't want to sound too strident here, but that kind of "protection" is going to hamstring our teenage sons in the rough and tumble of life. We dads need to know that our boys are becoming *men* of God and not *women* of God. We need to consciously and diligently work to strengthen them lest they become "mamma's boys." Obviously there is no merit in raising harsh boys who have not learned the power of gentleness. But neither is there any merit in raising soft sons who are not strong enough to confidently take their place among the men of this world. We have got to cut our boys loose from their mothers' apron strings!

"It is by his deeds that a lad distinguishes himself, if his conduct is good and right."

- Proverbs 20:11

Public school can be a great training ground to help our youth understand that they are on a genuine mission to save their world. One of our movement's earliest dads (and now one of its earliest granddads and great-granddads!), Herschel Martindale, has said it best: "All of our sons and daughters are either missionaries or a mission field." Our sons and daughters must each learn to stand for Christ and to be His witness – and not always under the protective arm of a parent.

I desire that each of us would have a clear vision of the realities ahead for our children, that we might train them diligently with an eye toward releasing them with faith and confidence. Even if our kids are still at home somewhat later in life, we need to have proven confidence in them that they will do well when they leave.

We cannot afford to be "barn blind" when it comes to assessing our kids. A barn-blind shepherd thinks that his sheep are perfect and he fails to see their faults clearly. He surely loves his sheep, but in order to choose what's best for them, he must also know them through and through and be able to "judge" them, as it were, fairly and impartially.

Sometimes we are not as objective as we need to be in judging the effect of our own ministry at home. We could benefit from the judgment of a trusted fellow dad in assessing how we're really doing in raising our 10- and 15-year-olds.

I would encourage each of you men to take advantage of this kind of counsel. Encourage a fellow dad that you respect and trust to be candid with you. Ask him, "How am I doing? How are my children doing? Are they able to stand against the pressures of this world? Are they able to work and relate and compete in this world, while running according to their King's rules?

"My father would have enjoyed what you have so generously said of me – and my mother would have believed it."

- Lyndon B. Johnson

I am confident that just as we have laid good foundations in the lives of our younger children, we will excel with our teens in their preparation for life and their release. But I want us to stay ahead of the curve. Regrets within a man's home can fundamentally weaken his work and ministry outside his home.

Brothers, if I could summarize my concern and counsel for all of us – myself included – I would graciously implore each of us to be strong, to be firm, and to be clear-eyed in the evaluation of our sons' and daughters' progress toward adulthood.

I want you parents to learn from my mistakes, so that when you make mistakes - and you will make mistakes – you can make brand new ones of your very own.

Releasing our "arrows"

We all have read the psalmist's analogy comparing our children to arrows.

For those of you not familiar with archery, an archer physically "trains" an arrow long before hunting season. It is tempered, planed, polished and painted. In Bible times, when arrows weren't mass-produced the way they are today, each arrow was unique. Back then, an archer who was "training" an arrow also needed to shoot it a few times to test it and see how it would handle when released in the heat of the hunt. The skillful archer never truly releases an arrow until it is fully "trained," until he is confident that it will hit the mark.

We must treat our spiritual "arrows" the same way. We must continue to train our sons and daughters until we are confident that they can hit the mark. I cannot stress this strongly enough, parents. _Do not release them until it is time!_

I have never released my son or daughter until he or she has physically moved out of my house and gone off to college. As long as they live under my roof, I am coaching and directing them. I have never handed them over to their peers under the false, spiritualized notion that they are "just trying to reach the world." Are they really trying to reach the world – or are they just being pulled away?

Here's a practical example of how this plays out in the Whitney household. Our kids have never had a "right" to be out on Friday and Saturday nights, where they are automatically allowed to be gone every evening of every weekend. Instead we talk about their options and their choices each week.

(Just as an aside, I can't understand how parents can have no idea where their kids are and still keep their sanity. That's why lately I've taken to showing those public service ads in our parenting seminars – you know, the ones aimed at parents that say, _"Ask: Who? What? Where? When?"_

Of course, as we get older, more and more of us are beginning to release that first arrow. Some of us have released our second and third arrows. Some of you, like Neva and I, have released even more arrows. It is an inevitable part of parenting. Eventually, each of us will have to empty that quiver and release all of our arrows out into the world.

After all of this preparation, after all of this training, when the moment of truth arrives, *how* we release our arrow is critical to its success. We must release our arrow in such a way that it hits its mark, that it succeeds in the purpose for which it was launched.

We all want our sons and daughters to live a full and meaningful life. For most of them, that life will involve career and marriage – life both outside and inside the home. Will they put in the effort to get the training they need to secure the employment that will enrich their lives? Are they disciplined enough to make good marriage partners? In these two major areas, their character, maturity and leadership will be tested and revealed.

We can be confident that if our sons and daughters have a good reputation with those outside the church, coupled with relational and management skills inside the home, they will be fit for life.

"In place of your fathers will be your sons; You shall make them princes in all the earth."

- Psalm 45:16

"I believe that the greatest need for being a successful parent, it to have strong hearts and strong willpower."

Chapter 10 – Discussion Questions

1. Concerning hard work, are you an example to your children? Do you find yourself complaining about your job or about tasks around the house?

2. Often it is less work (in the short run) to simply do a task at home ourselves rather than ask one of our children to do it. How often do you find yourself doing this?

3. How can you train your children, especially if they are in their teens, to stand out in their reputation?

4. Ask another dad you respect how you are doing as a dad.

11
From "Gerbers" to the Glory of God

"I have no greater joy than to hear of my children walking in the truth."

- 3rd John 1:4

Author's note: My kids have grown since I wrote this chapter several years ago, but I wanted to use these "war stories" to help us envision our youth living out the Great Commission in their lives right now. So here is a recap of a recent year in the life of the Whitney clan.

Tonight my daughter should get back from a two-week short-term mission trip to Honduras. After only the first week, I have heard encouraging reports – many amazing stories and over 100 people saved. They walked into one university classroom and the whole class prayed to receive Christ! I'm sure that Steve Nelson - our pastor from Greeley who led the team - is pumped!

My oldest is already at Estes Park for our association's summer Leadership Training (LT) program. He is at the front desk checking people in, so you can't miss him. He came home last Saturday to see his sister Joy graduate from high school. Another one out the door and off to the races. She too is working at the front desk at a new hotel near the airport this summer and she absolutely loves it.

My upcoming sophomore has started her two summer jobs. (I guess they take me seriously when I tell them that they are on their own dime!) She is still thrilled to have lettered in track as a freshman. She ran in a few relays and also some hurdle events. I guess those long legs helped.

My 13-year-old son took it very seriously when a neighbor called him to see if he could work outside with them this summer building fence, clearing brush, digging postholes and generally just sweating like a horse. "You bet!" he said. So there he is.

My two youngest daughters – "Thelma" and "Louise" – are just busy being young girls. They are doing a few more chores and playing and working with their 4-H projects and talking and playing and…

I was thinking about this last school year the other day. It seems like we always think about our families when work isn't pressing and our minds are free to wander. Funny how you can be very busy but then, when you're idle for a minute, your thoughts often turn to your kids or to your wife. Kind of like a compass needle homing back in on true north.

I was thinking about what has blessed me most in their lives this last year.

These are my memories:

My youngest and last "heathen" finally got saved this last year. She had been anxious about being the only pagan at the dinner table and had been pestering us about becoming a Christian for quite awhile.

On the way home from church one Sunday, I happened to look in the rear-view mirror and saw her crying. "What's wrong, Beck?" I asked.

"Dad, I was trying to make peace between my two best friends in Sunday school," she said, "but I just couldn't do it." (Apparently there was a little tiff between a couple of her friends.)

"I know there is a verse about 'Blessed are the peacemakers,' but I just couldn't make them get along," she sobbed. "I couldn't get them to make up with each other either."

I looked at her in the mirror again and told her how it's pretty hard to do something like that without Christ. "Honey, maybe it's time for you to accept Christ," I suggested.

When I looked in the mirror again, every female in the car was crying!

I asked, "Why are you all crying now!?" They said they were "just happy," but Becca was the most thrilled of all.

She said, "I'm crying now because you said that I can become a Christian."

So anyway, driving down the road, in the car, on the way home from church, she prayed to receive Christ right there in front of her whole family. When she finished, the next words out of her mouth were, "Can I call Josh and Mandy at CSU and tell them what happened? Can I call both grandmas and tell them?"

When she got home, she immediately made her phone calls. I listened in when she called my mom. It was pretty interesting:

"Guess what, Grandma!?" Becca said. "I just became a Christian!"

To which my mom answered, "That's sweet, honey, but you've always been a Christian. You are my little darling."

"No, Grandma," Becca insisted, "I just accepted Christ!"

"That's wonderful, honey," my mom said. "Could I talk to your dad?"

I got on the line and my mother said, "What's going on, Rick? She's always been such a dear granddaughter. What have you said to her?"

Well, how would you answer your mom if she asked you that?

I said the most courageous thing I could think of: "I don't know, Mom. Here, talk to Becca again."

Rebecca took the phone and said for the third time now, "Really, Grandma, I just became a Christian! In the car, on the way home from church!"

Another one – my last one – "bites the dust." My work is through.

That was a good memory.

Another good memory was when my daughter who's a senior got to lead the two girls she's been babysitting for years to the Lord. The youngest, who is handicapped and uses crutches, met my daughter one Saturday night with this question, "Joy, what's hell like?"

"Why are you worried about hell, Madi?" Joy responded. "Listen, I'll tell you about heaven and hell – and I'll tell you again how you can accept Christ if you'd like me to."

So Joy did and Madi prayed and the first thing Madi did was wrap her arms around herself and shout, "He's in me!" Then very seriously she asked, "Joy, if I fall down, will He fall out?" (Since she is physically handicapped, falling down occurs quite often.)

"No, Madi."

"Joy, could anyone in my family do this and pray and become a Christian?"

"Yes, Madi."

"Joy, could anyone on our street pray and become a Christian?"

"Yes, Madi."

"Joy, could anyone in Brighton pray and become a Christian?"

"Yes, Madi."

"Joy, why *wouldn't* they?!"

Then just a few weeks later, on another Saturday night babysitting assignment, Madi's older sister met Joy at the door with this statement: "Tonight I want to become a Christian, if you will go through that bridge diagram again." So Joy did and Codi did.

The next week Codi had to give a speech before her class on the topic of "Something Exciting That Has Happened to Me." Codi asked to use the blackboard and opened her speech with this sentence: "I used to think I was a Christian, like many of you. But I wasn't. Now I am. This is how I got saved."

Codi then proceeded to explain the bridge diagram and ended her speech with this sentence: "If any of you have any questions, talk to me after class."

She told Joy all about it the following week, asking, "Did I do the right thing, Joy?"

Anyway, Molly, the mother of these two girls, has gotten pretty interested in spiritual things. After going to a Women's Breakfast Club at church, Joy and Neva got to share with her at some length. She had several honest questions she was struggling with and just the other day she stopped by and talked with Neva and I for over an hour about the condition of her soul and yet her joy in knowing that her daughters are saved.

She is reading through the gospel of John and has said that she will never forget Joy crying over her not being saved. She confessed to us that she has been deeply moved to do something about her questions, saying, "I feel that God is surrounding me."

These were such encouraging memories for my family. (Why do adults make things so difficult? Why can't we just exhibit childlike faith like these kids?)

Molly said that both her daughters are sharing the gospel with their friends. Apparently one of the girls wanted a friend to come over and was trying to synchronize the visit for the same night that one of my daughters was scheduled to baby-sit.

"Why, Madi?" asked Molly.

"Well, my friend Angelo needs to get saved, Mom," Madi said.

The other daughter went through the cross diagram with all of the youth while she was babysitting for a neuro-fibromatosis meeting in the basement of a local Mormon church. That got her mom into a little hot water, but even so Molly said she was proud of her daughter.

Over this last year, Josh and Mandy have each seen many of their college friends saved, then worked to build the friendships even more, and have brought some of these new Christians home to spend a night here. It seems like we have had ten or more of their friends at one time here with us for Thanksgiving and Christmas and Easter and quite a few other weekends in between.

Each salvation story of all these different college students has been unique and their testimonies around our dinner table were encouraging – but they were especially encouraging - when I saw the twinkle they put in my college kids' eyes.

This Kingdom building with your kids is great stuff.

"Do we parents see raising our kids as one major way to

help fulfill the Great Commission? We must!"

- John Meyer, fellow dad

Recently Neva has been very encouraged by what the Lord has done in her family. For over 30 years she has prayed for her brothers and sisters and their families. Here are two quick stories on how God has begun answering her prayers.

Neva's niece Rachel went off to Iowa State University as a freshman last fall. The Colorado State University cousins got after the ISU Christians at the Myrtle Beach LT program last summer and encouraged them to go love this cousin. So they did.

After spending a few months getting to know the guys and gals, hearing quite a bit about the Gospel, and then spending a tearful Sunday afternoon talking to God in a cemetery, Rachel got saved.

She immediately e-mailed Neva and expressed her gratitude. "Aunt Neva, thank you so much for praying for me and my family all these years," the email read.

Rachel got baptized at the Spring Student Banquet in front of her folks and has been sharing her faith with her family. Now she is out here in Colorado for the summer LT program at Estes Park. Rachel and her newfound heart cause Neva to cry almost every time she thinks of her.

Another one of Neva's nieces came to the Kitacki Spring Teen Conference last month here in the Northwest region. This sweet girl, Jenny, sent in our very first registration for the conference with the following note: "Uncle Rick, I sure hope there is still room for me." (Her registration was followed by 350 other tardy ones, but that is another topic.)

Anyway, she came, prayed to receive Christ with my daughter Grace on Saturday night and hugged everyone she could on Sunday morning with the words, "He's in me!"

Just this week Jenny wrote my daughter: "Guess what, Grace? God used me! I was reading my Bible on the bus last week and one of my friends asked me about it and I ended up sharing that diagram you went through with me and do you know what? She got saved!" And she started crying, then I started crying. I love the Lord so much."

Her letter encouraged all of us here at the Whitney homestead. (Man, we sure do a lot of crying around here!)

Then last Saturday night we had our end-of-the-school-year Teen Burger Bash. Almost all of the 20 youth in our church brought at least one friend. After demolishing the hamburgers, the teens shared testimonies and sang and went over the gospel diagram and handed out copies of the book of John and gospel tracts entitled Do You Know for Certain?

Two of Grace's classmates were there. When they met her at school the next week, they told her they wanted to pray the prayer but that they had a few questions. Grace sat with them at lunch and answered their questions all week. Questions like, "I know I will probably blow it and sin next week after I pray with you. Will I still be saved?" And, "Grace, do you mean that my mom and dad could also pray this?" And, "Where is that verse 'By grace are you saved through faith and that not of yourself, it is the gift of God, not of works?' I can't find it in the booklet you gave me."

"That's the heart of it, isn't it, Grace?"

Anyway, after answering their questions all week, Grace told them to get ready, because to pray is a serious thing and that if they still wanted to get saved tomorrow during lunch, then she would pray with them. That night Grace told a couple of believers at school that she was pretty sure that Katy and Krista were going to accept Christ the next day. "When they do and I bring them across the lunchroom tomorrow," Grace said, "be sure to tell them what you think of their decision."

Sure enough, that next day they prayed to accept Christ.

Grace immediately asked them "What do you say to someone when they have given you a gift?" They both answered, "You thank them."

"What do you think you should say to Christ, now that He has given you the gift of eternal life?" Both of these girls immediately bowed their heads and thanked the Lord for saving them.

Grace led them over to the other Christians and with squeals and tears they all rejoiced. Quite a high school lunch hour!

The girls are beginning to go through a Bible study for new Christians, and they each want to go through that gospel booklet with their parents.

(Neva and I heard this story over the phone last week, while we were away for a few days celebrating our 25th wedding anniversary.)

Anyway, these are a few of the "glory stories" that have encouraged me and filled my heart lately. Stories about sharing the gospel are the best stories in the world for our youth. They are the stuff of life. It motivates me beyond expression when I experience how God can use our kids to work alongside us as co-laborers in the gospel.

This is not just a way of living for certain "special" families. I hope you have caught the vision that this can eventually be a reality in each of our families if we'll just stick it out, if we'll just stay the course and remain strong and expectant in our faith as we help our youth weather the storms of adolescence.

John Meyer, a good friend, has said the following concerning this working together in our families to see His Kingdom advance.

"We are called to make disciples and by far the greatest

opportunity we will ever have is discipling our children. We get access to them for eighteen years, we get almost exclusive access to them for five to ten years. They come with no preconceived world view and God has created their relationship with us to be the most influential they will ever experience. Soooo, if we cannot effectively pass on our faith and our concern for the lost, to our children, either we have not realized we are supposed to do so, or we don't really have a vibrant relationship with the Lord ourselves. This may sound a little strong, but I believe it's true."

He goes on to share one specific way that he tries to carry out the Great Commission in his family. *"One thing I do is try to find things we can be responsible for as a family, that somehow impacts people for Christ."*

I finally saw the movie The Horse Whisperer the other night. In the film, the daughter is fighting against her mother and the mother is hesitant to impose her will. Should she pursue her daughter or back off?

In an important scene, our cowboy hero Tom Booker turns to the mother and says, *"Don't let her turn you away."* The cowboy's words are also for us. We need to stick with it.

We can each have a whole litany of family stories to recount each year as our kids get older and older – exciting, personal stories of how they each helped fulfill the Great Commission – but it will never happen if we let them turn us away.

Dads, we need to take the reins and make sure that our kids spend a lot of time together with us being "on mission" as a family. (We had better make it a lot of fun, too, if you hope to keep it up year after year!) If we do, in time we will reap amazing, eternal rewards.

Serving God and working to see his Kingdom advanced is

challenging and exciting and thrilling and heartbreaking and frustrating all at once. It's the best business in the world – and there's no finer way to do life on this temporary piece of ground than to work side by side with your kids for the sake of the Kingdom!

Chapter 11 - Discussion Questions

1. Do you need training in how to share your faith with someone?

2. If you have teens, do they need training?

3. How can you have your whole family participate together in helping win friends and neighbors and people you know - to Christ?

12
How Are They Stacking Up?

When we are looking for a potential leader, we usually start with a guy who is pretty friendly, who is also good company, and who is easy to be around. He often shows real ability at work, at home, and in his church.

But if we are evaluating his ability to lead people, there's one specific attribute that makes him stand out. Because of our early history as a movement of churches and our own unique "spiritual genetic code," when we see this quality in a man we immediately take note of him. He may have some weaknesses in his life, but if we see success in this one area – and especially if we see it over and over – any doubts we might have about his leadership tend to be alleviated.

Have you guessed it yet? The attribute I'm talking about is the ability to speak for Christ, to see people saved, and to see them join us in God's cause.

If someone is able to clearly communicate the gospel and lead people to Christ – whether it's a neighbor or a friend at work

– we are impressed. While we recognize the importance of spiritual gifts and know that gifts (grace) differ between believers, we are especially impressed when we see a man speak up and win someone to Christ and to the church.

Because we know that what's on this man's heart is what's on God's heart – reaching the lost!

If a person never seems to see anyone get saved, we eventually begin to wonder:

- Does he believe in sharing the gospel?
- Does he have enough courage and discipline to speak for Christ – with gentleness, but with initiative?
- How solid is his walk with Christ?
- How well does he understand his position in Christ and why we are redeemed, yet still left here on this earth?

Each of us is involved in the gospel, whether we like it or not. Although our own spiritual gifts vary, we all take joy when we are used by God in the salvation of others. When we see someone saved, we always share it – either in conversation or in our teaching – to encourage others, to stimulate our Christian brothers and sisters to greater works.

We also believe that to eventually see someone saved is evidence of a kind of balance in a person's Christian life. For instance:

- When we know that we are forgiven, it affects both our speech and our behavior. If we truly know that we are forgiven, we are filled with a joy that just naturally spills out of our lives. We almost cannot help but speak for Christt.
- Knowing what Christ has done for us strengthens our view of who we are. A person with a healthy, Christian self-image will naturally speak for Christ.

- When we recognize His lordship in our lives, we are able to place our emotions and fears under His control. We will then speak for Him in season or out, whether it "feels" emotionally convenient or not.

My point in all of this is to ask you a question. *Do you believe that evangelism is a mark of genuine spiritual health in your teenager's soul, as well as in your own?* I hope you do.

Years ago I read an amazing statistic that demonstrates to me how an enthusiasm for evangelism is a good barometer for gauging spiritual health.

Do you know that it takes approximately 10,000 families here in America to produce one child that will make it into the pages of Who's Who? That's right, it takes 10,000 families (and all of their kids!) to get one child who does something remarkable enough to land in the book.

But do you know how many *missionary* families it takes to produce a child that will land on the pages of Who's Who? *Only nine!*

What I'm trying to say is that an evangelistic spirit seems to fundamentally qualify a young man or woman for a life of service. Our children's ability to successfully speak to others for Christ reveals a certain kind of spiritual health. It is a mark of something deeper going on inside.

Are our teens actually seeing their friends saved? Probably not every week or month, but are they successfully seeing their schoolmates come to Christ?

This litmus test has direct application in our homes, because it helps us to evaluate our kids' spiritual health in a host of areas.

Speaking the truth

When children are little, they say the craziest things. Art

Linkletter and Bill Cosby both took advantage of this on their TV shows all the time.

Little kids are funny and cute and have an amazing simplicity and directness. They just tend to speak the truth right out, and we are refreshed by their directness, even if they are only four years old. Let me illustrate with another story from the Whitney archives.

When the movie Jurassic Park first came out many years ago, we decided to all go see it as a family after church one Sunday afternoon. All seven of my children were younger and at home then, and my youngest daughter Rebecca was four.

Do you remember the scene where the two SUVs were tipped upside down at night and the two kids in one of the SUVs were fooling around with the flashlight? And T-rex was sniffing around and began to notice the flashlight and started turning towards the trapped children?

The theater was absolutely quiet, so still you could almost hear your heart beating. And then the scientist trapped in the other SUV whispered, "Turn off the light." He said it almost to himself really. Then he whispered it a second time, "Turn... off... the... light."

Well, right in the middle of that dark, packed, hushed theater – with everyone holding their breath for fear that the dinosaur would spot the kids – my youngest daughter stood up, grabbed the seat in front of her and screamed at the top of her lungs, "Turn off the light!"

Speaking the candid truth just seems to come naturally for young   kids. But with our teens, speaking the truth for Christ is a mark of maturity. In a season of life that is extremely peer-oriented, it demonstrates that they are putting what God thinks above what their friends might think. This says an awful lot about a teen's spiritual maturity.

Do they speak for their Savior? When they do speak for Christ, what's the result? Are they winning their friends to the faith with grace and patience – or clubbing them over the head?

We know that there are always areas where our youth are growing up in Christ, but when we see them successfully sharing their faith, we can be reassured that they are on the right track, on the right path.

What it reflects

There are several things we can surmise about our teens and their spiritual health if they are speaking for Christ:

- If they are speaking for Christ, they are growing in grace and are secure in their position in Christ. When you're secure in Christ, you will speak.
- If they are speaking for Christ, they are probably learning to discipline their emotions. They will be winning the "mood" battle. It is hard enough to speak for Christ on a good day, but it is especially difficult when you are self-absorbed or having a "pity party."
- If they are speaking for Christ, they are learning to put on a Christ-like countenance. This usually just means that they know how to smile and are actually doing it!
- If they are speaking for Christ – maybe not every day, but often – they are probably having a daily walk with God.
- If they are speaking for Christ, they probably have a good relationship with Mom and Dad.
- If they are speaking for Christ, I venture to guess that their academics are pretty good.
- If they are speaking for Christ, their discipline in sports, music, or other activities they're committed to will usually increase.
- If they are speaking for Christ, they are learning to win

the attitude battle. You can't be a spokesman for God and continue to "have an attitude." God tends to take care of His spokesman.

Here are some other things to think about as you assess your teen's spiritual maturity:

- Are they speaking for Christ whether or not it's their spiritual gift? Our sons' and daughters' spiritual gifts will vary just as ours do, but they must have some ability to organize what's on their heart and speak for Christ to their friends. And they should see some – not all, but some – of their friends saved. We're not all evangelists, but all of us are called to this good work of evangelism.

- Are they speaking about Christ to the lost or just with other Christian teens? Most any teen can "talk the talk" and share aspects of their faith with other Christian teens. That's the easy part. Christians are an incredibly tolerant lot, even teenage Christians. But the real measure of maturity is whether they're sharing their faith with their lost friends. We can't be confident in a teen if he never shares his faith.

- Are they speaking about Christ to the lost by themselves? The real measure of success is whether they demonstrate an ability to relate to and influence the lost when they are all alone, without all the cozy props of their Christian community. Can they deliver the truth to their peers in a winsome way – and are they taking the initiative to do it – even if no one else takes up the banner?

- Are they inviting their classmates to teen activities or outreach events? Just as we're encouraged when we see an adult bring a co-worker or neighbor to hear a special series of messages on Sunday morning, so too we're encouraged when our teens invite their friends to special events. One of our goals as parents in the training and equipping of our teenagers should involve helping them learn skills in inviting people and seeing them take the initiative in this area.

When children are younger we mostly deal with their behavior. When they become teens, it seems that we are mostly dealing with their attitude. There is one critical key to developing a good attitude in your teen – understanding that *good behavior leads to good attitude!*

Ask yourselves, what good behaviors are our teens demonstrating, day in and day out, in their Christian walk? Good behavior and habits in following the Lord naturally lead to a concern for the lost and the salvation of some.

Let me give you some examples from my own family.

I remember when my oldest, Josh, was just an incoming freshman in high school. It was early in the school year and he read about the idea of rallying at the flagpole and praying on a certain morning in September. He went that first year and only one other boy showed up. But he was still willing to stand up and be counted. Now hundreds of students take part.

What has blessed me even more than "See you at the pole" is seeing the Bible studies, prayer meetings and salvations that have followed as my children have spoken out for Christ over these many, many years. Each of my four collegians led classmates to Christ while still in high school. They started a prayer meeting on Monday mornings that is held in the central courtyard at the high school. They held breakfast Bible studies at the McDonalds before school. A lot of classmates have attended these gatherings. Everyone is talking about the stance of the Christians.

One of my daughter's friends sent her a note just last week

that said, "Thanks so much for sharing the Lord with me. Praying with you and receiving Christ has turned my life upside down. I love you."

My new college freshman was able to reach back and see a former high school classmate come to Christ just last week. For years my daughter Joy prayed for, witnessed to, and loved this girl; she never gave up. And now her friend has finally accepted Christ!

Parents, we can change the world beginning from our dining room table – through these kids we are raising!

I have mentioned stories before about the two families who are neighbors to us out here amongst the prairie dogs. They have come to Christ – the moms, the dads, the kids, everyone! And they are now doing the right thing and going to church. All of these salvations started through relationships with my teens.

Probably every one of you parents has similar stories. The point is, I want to encourage each of us to actually *have* salvation stories to tell. Then we can share them to encourage and stimulate other families to greater efforts in the gospel.

We must continue to work with our teens until we hear the gospel in their speech. If it is not in their words, it is not in their hearts. And if it is not in their hearts, then we know where our work must begin.

Most all of us are concerned about the impact that the world and the high school culture is having on our youth. The truth is, our children are either missionaries or a mission field – a fact that is forgotten by many Christian parents and is sadly lacking in many Christian parenting curriculums. The only way to make sure that our teens are wise and have the ability to keep their heads on straight is to give them a cause to live for.

Those of you with younger children have not faced this test yet. But it is a very real, spiritual litmus test for our teens. If they are speaking the truth in love and winning their friends to Christ, then we know that a number of good things are being built into their souls. If this is not happening, then we parents need to get to work.

I want to challenge you not to lower the bar in your expectations of your teens. Sure we love them and we'll always be patient with them. But do we still have grand dreams for our children?

I admit that I chuckled at my brother's joke: "When they were little, I dreamed that they would be champions for Christ. Now that they are sixteen, I will be glad if they are just law-abiding citizens." But I know that he hasn't settled for this with his teens. None of us can afford to.

"Let us see your miracles again; let our children see your glory at work. And may the Lord our God show us His approval and make our efforts successful. Yes, make our efforts successful!"

-Psalm 90:16,17

Quick thoughts on dating

In conclusion, let me touch briefly on dating and high school romances, those so-called "innocent friendships." Here's my only thought: *High school romances usually stunt our teens socially, intellectually and spiritually.* High school dating is a waste of time. I have found that if your kids are focused in and have a "prince among thieves" mentality, dating isn't really that big of a deal.

Don't worry, parents, they will find that special someone. Two of mine are married to beautiful mates. Their choices, as to wife and husband, have deeply pleased Neva and me.

You'll find an excellent article in the appendix entitled "Dating,

Romance and God's Will." It was written by Pat Sokoll, a fellow dad and a good friend. It's a challenging piece.

However, if the article doesn't grip you and your teenager still thinks she should be able to date, then following Pat's article is a handy form that you might want to copy off and use.

Perhaps you've seen it before. It's called "Application to Date My Daughter."

Chapter 12 – Discussion Questions

1. Even if your children are young, how can you begin cultivating in them a heart for non-Christians, those who do not yet know the Lord?

2. It is often said, "More is caught than taught." In other words, your children will *"catch"* as much or more from what you *"do"* as from what you *"say"*. Concerning your own actions in evangelism, what will your children *catch* from you?

3. What can you and your spouse do to grow in this area and to stretch your family?

13

When it's "Nose to Nose"

Q. Why was Abraham asked to sacrifice his son Isaac when he was about twelve years old?

A. Because when he turned thirteen, it wouldn't have been a sacrifice.

I just watched my fourth child head off to college. Grace has gone to "run her race."

But she was a handful her senior year in high school. She and I would butt heads often. We had many difficult showdowns where we would really get into it. And I would wonder, "Am I being too hard? After all, it's her senior year in high school."

On the one hand, I recognized that she was eighteen years old and ready to leave. On the other hand, I recognized that she was eighteen years old, still under my roof, and this was my last, best chance to influence her life. Our last year together.

Now don't get me wrong. Grace was a tremendous blessing. She is an incredibly hard worker, and in many ways we may not have had a church in Parker, Colorado, if it hadn't been for her help. She sang on Sundays and co-led the entire Sunday school for several months when we were just getting started. She helped me with all kinds of computer graphics and flyers. And I think she must have single-handedly set up at least 10,000 chairs over the past two years!

She was a very strong leader in our church youth group. She is very social and skilled at pulling people together. She got the teens working hard. She was probably the strongest leader I have ever raised for her stage in life.

Her peers voted her their Homecoming Queen. She was president of the National Honor Society. The faculty voted her the Outstanding Graduating Senior of her class last spring. The list went on and on.

But the truth is, Grace and I fought – a lot. It could get a little ugly at times.

Anyway, no matter how ugly things got, I would never yield to her unless she was right. I said that I was sorry at times when I would get angry, but I would never let her get her own way if she was wrong or if I just didn't think she should do something.

"I distrust any man (or woman) who claims to have had a continuous friendship with his father. How did they get from age 14 to 26?"

- Anonymous

She went off to college. And I worried.

I wondered if I had been too hard on her. Even dads who seem strong can still doubt themselves. I didn't hear from her and she didn't come home.

That public service ad on TV – the one that goes *"It's not pestering, it's parenting"* – gave me some measure of encouragement. I kept reminding myself that I was just doing my best. But two long months went by this fall. And then finally she sent us the following e-mail:

Dear Dad and Mom,

...Anyway, this is why I am writing. Mom and Dad, I want to ask for your forgiveness for my attitude at times during high school. Sometimes I wasn't very submissive or respectful and that was wrong of me. I think because I am so strong-headed at times it is hard for me to take correction. I feel like the Lord has really laid it on my heart to just change that and to really seek after Him.

It wasn't a good example to Mike, Jessica and Rebecca, because I was choosing to follow my flesh instead of God. That was sin and that was wrong.

As you both know, in the Bible it says honoring your parents is the first commandment with a blessing and I want to seek to just love and honor you two so much more. I think we have a WONDERFUL relationship, but I want us to have an EXCELLENT relationship.

Also, at times you were hard on me but it was for my own good, so thank you for that. I adore you two so much, Mom and Dad. I respect you both and strive to be more like you two. I know that I make you proud and I know that you love me. I know that you two forgive me for being silly, but I just wanted to be cleansed and pure of that sin of not always honoring my parents – in front of God and you two.

I am sorry, Mom and Dad, and I love you two, I respect you two and I ADORE you two with all of my heart. All of my heart. Also, I feel a little emotional right now, but I just wanted to share that with you...

Love, Grace

As I read her note, I could just picture her great big, dark eyes puddling up with tears. Here's what I wrote back:

Dear Princess,
Thank you for your sweet words, princess. We love you. We are proud of you. And we forgive you. We are confident that you will do well, babe.

> *Love,*
> *Dad*

I wanted to share this rather personal story to encourage you to <u>stay the course</u> with each and every one of your kids. We must not yield to our son's self-will or our daughter's whining just because we are tired or frustrated. And we must not subtly sidestep our parental responsibilities by shifting the blame for our inadequacies onto our teens, reasoning that we would automatically be better parents if only our teens were "more spiritual."

Even our Lord and His parents had communication problems. Remember when He stayed behind at the temple and His folks didn't know where He was. He obviously must not have told them. They asked Him why He took off like that. And His reply was, *"Didn't you know. . . .?"* This Scripture reveals that there is going to be that occasional generation gap, even in the best of families.

When they are little and young, we are looking for simple obedience. They are both a ton of fun and able to vex us at the very same time. When our children are young, those "spiritual Kodak moments" seem to pop up every week or two. But let's not be naïve. There isn't much weight or deliberation behind those highly quotable, child-like comments about God or life or us. Cute phrases may *sound* spiritual, but they are not the stuff of genuine spirituality. We know that it's not so much what our children *say* –

as what they ultimately choose to *do* – that demonstrates true spirituality.

That's why as parents we need to be primarily focused on building a foundation of obedience in our sons' and daughters' everyday lives. When they're just getting started in life, we begin teaching them to obey Mommy and Daddy. When they get to be 10 years old, we're still working on an obedient heart. And when they're teens, we still must be speaking to and insisting upon an obedient spirit. Even when there is resistance.

"The main purpose of holding children's parties is to remind yourself that there are children more awful than your own."

It drives me up a wall when I see a parent stymied by a teen who's displaying an attitude and doesn't want to pray or read his Bible or go to youth group or church. The parent usually says something to me like, "Well I sure don't want to make him do it if he really doesn't want to." What a weak, silly, stupid response on the part of us as parents! We would never carry that line of thinking over into whether they should go to school in the morning!

"We are given children to test us and make us more spiritual."

- George F. Will

With each of my teens, my wife and I have insisted on a certain caliber of speech and behavior while they lived under our roof. We wanted them not only to talk the talk, but to walk the walk – to live out their Christian convictions whether they felt like it or not. They needed to put on Christ, to use Christ-like speech and display Christ-like behavior and a Christ-like countenance – not only with people outside the family, but within our four walls as well.

By "insisting," I'm not talking about just *talking* to them. I'm talking about *training* them. Training means demonstrating, coaching, reminding – and continuing to demonstrate, coach and remind until there is real change and growth.

We have insisted on Christ-like behavior with each of our kids. And here's the best part: *We have gotten it from every one of them!*

"The most important thing in the world that makes young people civilized is good old people. There is a myth going around that young people today know more than their elders. The fact is that everything young people know, they learned from their elders."

-Anonymous

Pat Sokoll has mentioned that girls can often seem a little more spiritual than boys, but their spirituality may not be that real. Girls just like to talk more and express themselves and this can be misread as spirituality. I agree with him.

When we require them to run the way of God's Word and follow Him, over and over, month after month, year after year – whether they feel like it or not – eventually God breaks through and "enlarges their hearts" (Psalm 119:32). In my experience, this kind of genuine spirituality, the sort that springs from within, often comes later rather than sooner in our sons' and daughters' lives. It may be delayed. It may not show up until a few years down the road. But it always comes.

All of my kids who have left the nest and moved on to college have had a deeper realization, a time of decision, a season of soulsearching when they began "owning" their faith even more. With no parent there telling them what to do, alone before their God, they have determined on their own to repent and grow in certain areas. (Kind of like when God got hold of many of our hearts at that same stage in life.)

That's why it's so crucial that we don't give in or give up when it comes to insisting on right behavior. So much of their future hangs in the balance. We must not let ourselves be dissuaded or derailed simply because we don't see the best of hearts in our teens right now. We cannot let our teens get away with an attitude.

The worst thing we can do is to let them get away with an attitude.

"Don't give me that attitude, girl!" You may want to memorize these words.

No matter how difficult the tension might be between any son or daughter and mom or dad, we parents need to stay firmly engaged. It is for their future. We cannot yield. We must hunker down and "stay the course."

In the introduction to this book I mentioned how one of my daughters once stood before me with her hands on her hips and declared with all the passion she could muster, *"Dad, sometimes I don't think that you love me!"* And I could read her eyes and saw her anger and knew that she probably just wanted to blurt out, *"Dad, I hate you."*

What do we do then? When the kids are angry and say things, have you ever felt like two or three arrows have just pierced your gut or your heart? What do we do?

Well, first we emotionally need to pause a second, take a deep breath and pull out the arrows. Then we need to respond. What I said was, *"Honey, you know I love you."* and, *"No, you still can't do what you want to do."*

When the kids get super emotional, it is usually because they just want something. We can not afford to respond in kind. We need to get control. But this is critical – *we must not yield to their demands,* even when they threaten and say things they might not feel. This is where many parents wilt and fail before the onslaught.

At times it will feel like we are almost forcing them to display Christ-like behavior. But we need to be tenacious, even though things can seem pretty rocky at times. Let me close this chapter by illustrating the kind of no-matter-what tenacity we need with a story taken right from the headlines.

Some years ago on a hot summer day in south Florida, a little boy decided to cool off with a quick swim in the lake out behind his house. So he ran out the back door – leaving a trail of shoes, socks, and a T-shirt in his wake – plunged right in and began swimming towards the middle of the lake.

Back in the house, his mother happened to look out the window. To her horror she saw an alligator starting to close in on him from the center of the lake.

In utter terror, she ran toward the water, yelling to her son at the top of her lungs. When he heard her yelling, he became alarmed, instantly made a U-turn in the water and began swimming back toward his mother.

But it was too late. Just as he reached his mother, the alligator reached him.

From the dock she grabbed her little boy by the arms just as the alligator snatched his legs. Then ensued an incredible tug-of-war between the two. The alligator was much stronger than the mother, but the mother was much too passionate to let go.

A farmer driving by heard her screams, raced from his

truck and shot the alligator. Miraculously the boy survived, but he spent many weeks in the hospital recovering from his wounds. His legs were extremely scarred by the vicious attack of the reptile. And his arms were marked with deep reminders of where his mother's fingernails had literally dug into his flesh in an effort to hang on to the son she loved.

A newspaper reporter who interviewed the boy after the event asked to see his scars. At first, the boy lifted his pant legs.

Then with obvious pride he said to the reporter, "But look at my arms. I have great scars on my arms, too. I have them because my Mom wouldn't let go."

Chapter 13 – Discussion Questions:

1. An important quote from this chapter is, *"The worst thing we can do is let them get away with an attitude."* In what circumstances do you need strength to *"stay the course?"*

2. Do you insist they "walk the walk" even when they don't feel like it (and even when you don't feel like it)?

"I believe that the greatest need for being a successful parent, is to have strong hearts and strong willpower."

14
Tough Talk about Teen Ministry

While many of us are not directly involved in teen ministry, we are all heavily involved in *parent ministry*. It is our responsibility as fathers and mothers to train our youth. Therefore, it is crucial that we be significantly involved in providing ongoing, hands-on direction to our teens' youth ministries.

Josh McDowell, who has probably spoken to more college students about Christ than any other man alive, is simply adamant about this.

"I would fire all of the church youth pastors in this country," he said. "Form a dads committee. Then rehire those same youth pastors to work for the dads. And help train and equip our youth, under the fathers' guidance and supervision."

There's a boatload of wisdom in what he says. I have my own strong opinions on the topic of parents and teen ministries. I believe there are five common approaches to youth ministry that ultimately destine it to failure, no matter how well intentioned the goal. The good news is, failure doesn't have to be an option. I believe the solution is simple: significant parental involvement, particularly involvement by fathers.

Here then are those five misguided approaches, followed by my opinions on each. I want to stress at the outset that my opinions are just that: *opinions*. (But then I want to stress that there's a lot of hard-earned, school-of-hard-knocks experience behind those "opinions" – experience in successfully fathering and pastoring many teens and in mentoring many other fathers and pastors of teens – so I hope you'll hear me out!)

1. Any youth or teen ministry that does not involve dads in a critical leadership role is destined to fail.

John Meyer and I were recently talking about the different kinds of dads that we often see in Christian community. They seem to fall into three categories:

- Great dads have great expectations for their kids.
- Average dads have average expectations for their kids.
- Many dads just don't want to be bothered.

Dads, we cannot afford to be like the guy who just doesn't want to be bothered with being involved with his teens. (Kind of like when we didn't want to be bothered with a dirty diaper.) Well, we could avoid the issue then, but we can't avoid it now. Now that our kids are older, we just can't ignore reality and run off to the office. The chickens have a way of "coming home to roost," as they say. We need to have great expectations for our sons and daughters and to actively see that they live up to their potential with all that is in us.

Let's face it – we parents basically see our kids 24/7. We know how they're *really* doing. We know how they act when they get up in the morning and what they're like when they're in one of their moods. We're the main recipients of their stinky attitudes – that is, right up until they "pull their act together," hop out of the car all smiles and run off to see their friends.

Because we parents know the real score, we have the best opportunity to help our kids. That's why it's critical that we dads are actively involved in teen ministry, lest we passively encourage a kind of hypocrisy in our teens.

There is nothing better than a group of dads leading together the youth of a church. Of course we will always welcome and work with quality college age men and women who desire to work with teens. But it is so much healthier for those young college age men and women to be working under the direction and supervision of a *"committee of dads."*

Since all successful teen ministry must ultimately connect with the parents of those teens - we need to stand ready as dads, and not just sit on the sidelines. We need to initiate and get involved, lest we become a critic. And we parents are the best ones to help build connections between these two age groups.

2. Any youth or teen ministry that smacks of a homeschool-based model is destined to fail – especially if it ignores the mission of the church to reach people outside its circles.

Dads, we need to get our kids ready for the real world. They have to be able to "run with the big dogs," so to speak. We pray to be able to have an impact for Christ in our towns and cities – and the people in these same towns and cities, by and large, send their kids to the public high schools.

Our kids must be able to function effectively for God in the real world. That is, they must be able to keep their eyes on their Savior and keep their noses clean. Remain a witness. Maybe not a perfect witness, but a witness out there in this lost world. They must learn how to remain on mission without losing their own souls in the process.

Can our home-schooled youth handle the less-sheltered

environment of the public school? If not, we dads need to seriously ask ourselves, "Why not?" Then we need to buckle down and work overtime with them on specific areas they need to develop in until we're convinced that they have what it takes.

3. Any youth or teen ministry that relies excessively on older youth as leaders – without dads involved – is destined to fail.

Let's be honest, men. Twenty-year-olds make great "big brothers," but they can't be the point men. It's just too easy for someone barely past his teenage years, someone alone in leadership, to side with a teen against a parent – whether consciously or not.

We're all thankful for those committed Christian men and women in their 20's who are not only tremendous workers, but also tremendous examples to our teens. I personally rely on several of them for help in our youth ministry and I thank God for each of them. But we dads are the seasoned veterans. We are the ones who have the authority, the spiritual maturity and the life experience to help shape and guide the youth entrusted to us. We dads need to be the point men!

4. Any youth or teen ministry that does not have a strong emphasis on equipping our youth to share their faith with their peers in their high school is destined to fail.

Dads, we need to ensure that our kids are equipped to pass on their faith. Have our teens in high school learned to stand their ground, to reach out and make friends and to lead that occasional classmate to Christ? Can they speak about their faith one-on-one – and more importantly, *will* they do it?

Our kids are not really equipped if they are not sharing their faith one-on-one in natural situations like after school, over a coke, during the noon hour, etc. If we are relying solely on group activities in a church teen ministry context for our teen evangelism – and that is the extent of how we're "equipping" our youth – then we have failed.

Our teens need to see that when they are sharing their faith – seemingly all alone – they are stepping into a greater relationship, a very personal kind of relationship with their Savior. In those times, they are really *not* alone – God is with them and they are actually multiplying their lives into the lives of other people.

Just two nights ago, my daughter's classmate and her mother were killed in a tragic accident just a block from our house, right out here in the country. The next day another friend of my daughter – who was also a friend of the girl who was killed – prayed to receive Christ with my sophomore, right there after school.

There is nothing quite like having enough guts to speak about your faith to a peer one-on-one. When we're willing to speak for Him apart from the safety of our friends, it reveals who we really are. It separates the men from the boys, the women from the girls. There is no substitute for our teens having the fundamental perspective ingrained in their lives that they are God's workers in God's field – whether they are surrounded by likeminded peers or standing alone for their beliefs.

5. Any youth or teen ministry that does not involve a significant amount of service – one where our teens are asked to genuinely work hard and not just sit around and talk – is destined to fail.

Dads, we need to instill a strong work ethic in our kids. Do we insist that they work hard enough and long enough to know what it really means to break a sweat? Do we require genuine studying, where they are truly applying themselves with concentrated focus – whether they are smart or not? When we come together at church, are they right alongside us working and helping to build God's kingdom – or are they just watching? Are they serving their fellow man or just talking with their friends? Service is our Lord's way. He who chose to wash the disciples' feet demonstrated to us that serving is how His kingdom is truly advanced. Our youth need to "own" this truth, to internalize it. They need to understand that the kingdom of God is not advanced through mere talking. Our teens can easily believe the lie that all they need to advance God's kingdom is a microphone and an electric guitar. Nothing could be further from the truth. He is the one who promised that as we lose our lives on a daily basis in the service of others – we truly find life.

"But He said, 'On the contrary, blessed are those who hear the word of God, and do it.'"

– Luke 11:28

Pat Sokoll, commenting on a local church's responsibility to plan and think through their teen ministry, has said the following:

"It is very important to clearly define the outcome goals for your teen ministry. It is possible to have a teen ministry of 200 plus teens attending weekly, see several, or even dozens saved every year, get rave reviews from students and many parents, and still be a failure. Success and failure must ultimately be decided according to the specific goals that the fathers have decided on."

"If a student ministry is church-based and designed to help parents bring their teen age children progressively to full maturity, the outcomes must reflect a balanced, Biblical goal - for their conduct and character. Excitement, cultural relevance and even numerical fruit must be kept in careful

balance with the primary goal of helping students understand, embrace and live out biblical truths, commands and convictions."

He goes on to state a few specific outcomes that he is working to see established in the lives of his local church's teens.

- Be in healthy relationships with the authorities in their lives.
- Relate to and appreciate all ages and levels of maturity – especially in their own family and with their own siblings.
- Empower them to own and contribute to the larger vision of the local church.
- Respect and look to those who are older in the faith.
- Have the attitude and actions of a producer, rather then a consumer.
- And understand and embrace the Core Values of our association of churches.

Here are three questions I pose to every parent. Neva and I have each had to search our heart with these three questions, many times.

A. Do we want to win? (with every child)
B. Are we willing to do whatever it takes?
C. Will we allow ourselves to be turned away?

While we're on the topic of teen ministries, I just want to interject a thought about insisting on right behavior. As many of you know, our movement has a strong and vibrant heritage of successfully reaching young people for Christ. Many of you reading this book right now are products of that exceptional vision and focus. In fact, many of you first embraced Christ yourselves in your teen years or early 20's because of the dedicated witness and exemplary life of one of your peers in Great Commission.

As a movement, we have always "set the bar high" in our

commitment to exhibit right behavior in all of our relationships, whether we're with our friends, our parents, our professors, our employers, or members of the opposite sex.

However, with so many new teens coming through our doors and swelling the ranks of our youth ministries – young teens from dysfunctional homes who don't share our standards – it can be tempting to relax a bit from insisting on right behavior in order to be more "winsome." Nothing could be farther from the truth! Youth group is exactly the place where we should be reminding everyone – teens and parents alike – about our standards and guidelines on proper behavior, especially between the guys and the gals. Because our society has such low standards, that is all the more reason why we need to be training God's high standards into our youth at every opportunity. We can keep the bar high and still be gracious and effective with newcomers. If anything, the high level of respect in our relationships will make the Gospel even more attractive.

On fun, friends and free time

As long as we're on the topic of right behavior, let me ask you a question. Why are we giving our teens so much free time to be with their friends, even their Christian friends?

It takes a lot of time for kids just to go to school and study and get their grades. I'm convinced that the biggest mistake many parents make when their teens get a little older is to let them walk out the front door way too often.

The bottom line is, if we want our children to excel in school and be prepared for the future, they're going to have to do their homework – whether it comes easy for them or not. And we're going to have to limit their school activities and, yes, sometimes even their church activities. They can't do everything.

Many times I've been asked, "How often do you let your

kids leave the house? How many activities are they involved in?" My first reaction is to feel a little defensive, because I haven't let them be out and about that much.

"But what about their school friends?" parents ask. "What about their Christian friends? What about church activities and youth group?"

Like I said, I can feel defensive at times.

But if we want our kids to get ahead in life, we will insist upon building a strong work ethic into them during their high school years. Life is primarily a lot of hard work, and we can encourage a real passion for work or we can just let them be lazy. The comic strip Zits is one of my favorites, but the teenage boy who is the central figure is probably the laziest young guy I have ever laughed at. We can't afford to be raising comic strip characters.

"Fatherhood has been known to transform even the toughest and most resilient into a quivering mass."

- Marcus Jacob Goldman

Many teen ministries in America today rely on excessive amounts of fun to keep youth engaged. We need to guard against this kind of "fun first" thinking that can gradually seep into our own thinking and homes.

"Ah, we just need to let them have fun while they're young," some folks say. Well, I consider myself a fun-loving kind of guy. (How did Steve Martin and Dan Akroyd put it in that skit they used to do many years ago? "We're just a couple of wild and crazy guys!")

Well, we Whitneys are too. I sure don't need to work at encouraging my kids to let loose and have fun. That comes pretty naturally to this bunch. Every member of the Whitney clan has his or her own wild and crazy side.

But as parents we have to resist the notion that our chief purpose in life is to make sure that our kids are happy. On the contrary, our chief purpose in life as it relates to our kids is to make sure that they succeed in these growing-up years and become productive Christian adults.

"My father gave me the greatest gift anyone could give another person. He believed in me."

- Jim Valvano, former <u>North Carolina State</u> basketball coach

For further study:

In the appendix are two additional pieces, outlining a typical, church-based, <u>father-led</u>, teen ministry. The first is entitled, **Purpose, Plan, and Standards**. It is a one-page document and highlights the main elements for what I believe constitutes a successful, high school, church-based, father-led, teen ministry. The church is <u>Summitview</u> and it is located in Loveland, Colorado. They have an exciting teen ministry and a lot of dads are involved.

The second is entitled, **Plan of Action**. In a little more detail it reviews the five crucial elements of a successful church-based, <u>father-led</u>, high school teen ministry. This also is a very clear and doable plan. Both are pretty good. The example church here is <u>Prairie View Community Church</u> located in Parker, Colorado.

Chapter 14 – Discussion Questions

1. Are you giving your teen too much "free time" to be with their friends, even Christian friends? How do you gauge how much is too much?

2. How do you react to the following statement at the end of this chapter?
"...As parents we have to resist the notion that our chief purpose in life is to make sure that our kids are happy. On the contrary, our chief purpose in life as it relates to our kids is to make sure that they succeed in these growing-up years and become productive Christian adults."

3. From the chapter, discuss with your spouse the following three questions: Do we want to win? (with every child) Are we willing to do whatever it takes? Will we allow ourselves to be turned away?

15
Two Amazing Moms – their Spirit, their Home, their Results

"Whatever the family has done, it has done ably and nobly.
And much of the capacity and talent, intensity and character,
of the more than 1,400 of the Edwards family is due to Mrs.
Edwards."

–A.E. Winship, author of an exhaustive study of
the descendents of Jonathan and Sarah Edwards

Following are excerpts about the lives of two extraordinary
mothers – Susanna Wesley and Sarah Edwards. Taken from two
excellent older books – <u>Susanna, Mother of the Wesleys</u> by
Rebecca Harmon and <u>Married to a Difficult Man</u> by Elizabeth
Dodds – they detail the spirit and methods of two women who
focused on their responsibilities at home and in so doing, affected
the course of history. Their stories, example and practical instruction
are incredible, inspiring and well worth reading.

From <u>Susanna, Mother of the Wesleys</u>
-by Rebecca Harmon

Born in 1669, Susanna Annesley was the 25th child in her family. In 1690 she married Samuel Wesley, a country parson. She bore 19 children, of whom ten – three boys and seven girls – survived infancy.

She managed her large household through a carefully planned system of training for her children. In a 1732 reply to her son John's request for a precise account of her method, she writes:

Dear Son,

No one can, without renouncing the world, in the most literal sense, observe my method. There are few, if any, that would entirely devote above twenty years of the prime of life in hopes to save the souls of their children, which they think may be saved without so much ado; for that was my principal intention, however unskillfully and unsuccessfully managed.

According to your desire, I have collected the principal rules I observed in educating my family:

- *The children were always put into a regular method of living, in such things as they were capable of, from their birth; as in dressing and undressing, changing their linen, etc.*
- *(They were also trained) to bring them to a regular course of sleeping.*
- *They were never suffered to choose their food, but always made to eat such things as were provided for the family.*
- *Eating between meals was seldom allowed, unless in case of sickness, which seldom happened.*

- *The children were in bed by eight, and there was no such thing as sitting by a child until it fell asleep.*
- *They were so constantly used to eat and drink what was given them that when any of them as ill there was no difficulty in making them take the most unpleasant medicine.*
- *In order to form the minds of children, the first thing to be done is to conquer their will and bring them to an obedient temper. To inform the understanding is a work of time, and must with children proceed by slow degrees, as they are able to bear it; but subjecting the will is a thing which must be done at once, and the sooner the better, for by neglecting timely correction they will contract a stubbornness and obstinacy which are hardly ever after conquered, and never without using such severity as would be as painful to me as to the child. In the esteem of the world they pass for kind and indulgent whom I call cruel parents, who permit their children to get habits which they know must be afterwards broken. When this is thoroughly done, then a child is capable of being governed by the reason and piety of its parents, till its own understanding comes to maturity, and the principles of religion have taken root in the mind.*
- *When (they) turned a year old (and some before), they were taught to fear the rod, and to cry softly, by which they escaped abundance of correction which they might otherwise have had.*

In addition, this list was included in the letter:

1. *Subdue self-will in a child and thus work together with*

God to save his soul.

2. *Teach him to pray as soon as he can speak. Our children were taught as soon as they could speak, the Lord's prayer, which they were made to say at rising and bedtime.*
3. *Give him nothing he cries for and only what is good for him, if he asks for it politely.*
4. *To prevent lying, punish no fault which is truly confessed, but never allow a rebellious, sinful act to go unnoticed.*
5. *Command and reward good behavior.*
6. *Strictly observe all promises you have made to your child.*
7. *If ever any child performs an act of obedience, or did anything with an intention to please, though the performance was not well, yet the obedience and intention should be kindly accepted, and the child with sweetness directed how to do better for the future.*
8. *That the rights of property be invariably preserved.*
9. *That no boy or girl be taught to work till they can read very well.*

For their religious training she devised another basic system, that each child communicate to another what their mother had taught them. To each of the older children she devoted one evening for spiritual instruction. In addition, she gave all the children their academic training at home for six hours a day. "It is almost incredible what may be taught a child in a quarter of a year by a vigorous application, if it have but a tolerable capacity and good health."

In evaluating Mrs. Wesley's methods which now seem so hard and inflexible, we must remember that hers was a hard age, an age of harshness to children. The cruel floggings by tyrannical schoolmasters, as pictured by Dickens and other writers of a later period, were not exaggerated. "Strength guided by kindness," ruled in the Wesley household, and the love Susanna bore each individual child is evidenced by the fact that for many years she set aside a special time every week for each child. In a letter to his mother, John refers in tender terms to his Thursday evenings spent with her, wishing they could be continued.

Nowhere is there any record of resentment on the part of the Wesley children against their mother's method of education.

She was able to manage all her responsibilities through a carefully-ordered and very regular schedule, in which she allotted time each day not only for household chores, academic and religious training for her ten children, but regular devotions for herself as well. It is written of Mrs. Wesley that she withdrew from her duties for an hour, morning and evening, and also a shorter time at noon, to read and meditate on God's Word – which she claimed was "incomparably the best means to spiritualize our affections, confirm our judgment and add strength to our pious resolutions."

In spite of the fact that Mrs. Wesley's system of education runs counter to the tenets of modern child guidance experts, it is worthy of study because her method worked!

The children she reared developed into members of one of the most eminent families in English history, remarkable for their looks, their intellect, and their sterling character. Her daughters, though limited by their environment and the time in which they lived, were spirited and well educated. There was nothing craven about them. As for her three distinguished sons, the eminence they attained in their several spheres would never have been possible had they been "crushed" in spirit.

In her son John's journal it is written of the day she died that her last words were, "Children, as soon as I am released, sing a psalm of praise to God."

There can be no doubt that her regular method of living, according to a strict schedule and carefully-planned program designed to help her reach her goals, made a lasting impression on her sons John and Charles and contributed to the lifestyle which earned them the name "Methodists." In a very real sense, her training of her children contributed not only to the rise of the church movement her sons founded, but also the salvation of the societies of two nations, England and the United States.

From <u>Marriage to a Difficult Man</u>
-by Elizabeth Dodds
(The story of Sarah Edwards)

Sarah Edwards, wife of Jonathan Edwards, had an excellent way of governing her children. She knew how to make them regard and obey her cheerfully... in speaking to them she used gentle and pleasant words... She had to speak but once; she was cheerfully obeyed; murmuring and answering again were not known among the children.

In their manners, they were uncommonly respectful to their parents... when either parent was speaking... they were all immediately silent and attentive. The kind and gentle treatment they received from their mother, while she strictly and punctually maintained her parental authority, seemed naturally to promote a filial respect and affection, and to lead them to a mild, tender treatment of each other. Quarreling and contention, which too frequently take place among children, were in her family unknown.

She carefully observed the first appearance of resentment and ill will in her young children, towards any person whatever, and did not connive at it... but was careful to show her displeasure and suppress it to the up most; yet not by angry, wrathful words, which often provoke children to wrath... Her system of discipline was begun at an early age and it was her rule to resist the first, as well as every subsequent exhibition of temper or disobedience in the child... wisely reflecting that until a child will obey his parents, he can never be brought to obey God.

Jonathan Edwards, though an absent-minded father, gave his children another important thing: complete confidence that their parents loved each other. Sarah sat next to her husband at the table, and he treated her with great courtesy. She, in turn, leaned on him. It was written: "When she foresaw, or met with any special difficulty... she was wont to apply to her husband for advice and assistance and on such occasions they would both attend to it, as a matter of the utmost importance."

Sarah could count also on one hour a day when Edwards gave the family complete attention. He made sure to save an hour at the close of each day to spend with the children... The children knew they could save their questions and have their father's full attention at that precious hour when, without his wig and smoking his pipe, he was a different man from the one the parish usually saw. Although *Encyclopaedia Britannica* has chosen Edwards as the greatest mind America ever produced, with his children he was their dad.

In those days a father's place was unquestioned. The children were taught to fear their father, but not to quake before him. Edwards spoke from experience when he wrote: "As innocent as children seem to be to us, yet... they are naturally very senseless and ignorant, being born as the wild ass's colt, and need much to awaken them."

One source of the family stability was the steady, dependable routine of prayers which they had together, before breakfast and again after supper.

A mother's disciplinary role was uncomplicated by the Freudian insight then. Moreover, the entire social structure supported parental authority. A child who felt free to be insolent toward parents was as unthinkable in that society as was the internal combustion engine... Sarah's transactions with her children were reinforced because her husband treated her with total courtesy and serenely expected that each child would follow his example. A curious feature about the Edwards children is that the firmness did not squash individuality. One explanation for this may be found in a comment: "For (her children) she constantly and earnestly prayed and bore them on her heart before God... and that even before they were born."

That all the Edwards babies thrived in such precarious times is a comment on Sarah's instinctive sense of nutrition, her clean house, and her good health during pregnancy. This may have caused jealous twinges among other mothers in the town who were not so blessed.

The management of a large, busy household took leadership and efficiency. Mothers then had to be administrators, because the food and clothing depended on the mother's ability to produce it. Sarah had to learn to assign chores so that one child would take a turn breaking ice in the lean-to next to the kitchen, to get water for the breakfast tea, while another child brought in wood. Meanwhile, if a guest was leaving after breakfast, someone else would be packing lunch for his saddlebag. (A staple for such lunches was a "journey cake" - a cornmeal concoction.) Another girl would be setting the table.

Many households of that time were content to call a shot of hot buttered rum "breakfast," but the Edwardses sat down to large meals: bean porridge with ham bone, or cold corned beef and hot potatoes, or salt fish in cream. Cooking eggs was complicated because few houses had clocks. Eggs were sometimes timed by singing psalms. (An eight-line verse was usually right for boiling an egg.)

The cure for scurvy wasn't discovered until 1747, and this diet deficiency disease weakened many people, but there was none of it in Sarah's house. A prudent mother was also skeptical of drinking water. Many mothers found it safer to give babies beer, though one eighteenth-century almanac advised that it was "best to have their beer a little heated."

Children then had the advantage of knowing that their chores were indispensable. The smallest boy could help by watching a roast so that it browned evenly over fire. Chickens and geese had to be fed. Fires had to be kept going twenty-four hours a day, for there were no matches. If a fire was allowed to go out, it was necessary to borrow from a neighbor to avoid having to start it again by tediously scraping flint against wood.

The Edwardses saw that the children learned to be orderly about money. The family Bible contained a record of the savings of each child, with receipts, expenditures, and borrowings neatly recorded.

Sarah was "conscientiously careful, that nothing should be wasted and lost; and often, when she herself took care to save anything of trifling value, or directed her children to do likewise, or when she saw them waste anything, she would repeat the words of our Savior – that nothing be lost."

Sarah taught the girls to knit, embroider, and quilt. (Lucy once commented that making a quilt would be "very dull happiness to undertake alone.") They all took turns at the loom, and each girl seems to have developed her specialty in the housework. Esther gardened. Mary claimed she was the champion maker of chocolate. The family consumed this treat in such quantities that most of the Edward's shopping lists contained a reminder to buy chocolate. The house functioned efficiently because all of these highly individual children were taught to work together.

This is not to say that the household was idyllic. There were the normal clashes and jostlings of ego that might be found in any large family. Sarah, the oldest girl, was peppery. Mary, a black-eyed bundle of vivacity, had a short-fused temper and a piercing voice that could grate on the nerves. She had another weakness. She was terrified of thunderstorms, and would dive into a featherbed for the duration of the storm.

Quietly carrying the drudgery that freed her husband to study, Sarah Edwards also managed to train a brood of children whose social contribution is a phenomenon of American history. In 1900, A.E. Winship tracked down fourteen hundred of their descendants and published a study of the Edwards children in contrast to the Jukes family, the notorious clan who cost New York State a total of $1,250,000 in welfare and custodial charges. Jukes wasn't actually the name of the other family. The word means "to roost," and it was used about them because the family were social floaters, with no home or nest. They all originated with one immigrant who settled in upstate New York in 1720 and produced a tribe of "idleness, ignorance, and vulgarity."

Winship learned that a descendant of the Edwardses presided over the New York Prison Commission in 1874 when it conducted an inquiry into the Jukes matter. Only 20 of the 1,200 Jukeses had ever had gainful employment (the others were either criminals or lived on state aid), whereas the Edwards family had contributed astonishing riches to the American scene. "Whatever the family has done it has done ably and nobly," Winship contended. "And," he went on, "much of the capacity and talent, intensity and character, of the more than 1,400 of the Edwards family is due to Mrs. Edwards."

By 1900 when Winship made his study, this single marriage had produced:

- 13 college presidents
- 65 professors
- 100 lawyers
- 1 dean of an outstanding law school
- 30 judges
- 66 physicians
- 1 dean of a medical school
- 1 controller of the United States Treasury
- 80 holders of public office
- 3 United States senators
- 3 mayors of large cities
- 3 state governors
- 1 vice-president of the United States

Almost all the men had college degrees and many completed graduate work in a time when this was unusual. The women were repeatedly described as "great readers" or "highly intelligent," although the girls were not sent to college then. Members of the family wrote 135 books, ranging from "Five Years in an English University" to a tome on "Butterflies of North America." They edited eighteen journals and periodicals.

They entered the ministry in platoons and sent one hundred missionaries overseas, as well as stocking many mission boards with lay-trustees. One maverick married the daughter of a South Sea island chieftain but even that branch reverted to type, and its son became a clergyman.

As Winship put it: "Many large banks, banking houses and insurance companies have been directed by them. They have been owners and superintendents of large coalmines... of large iron plants and vast oil interests... and silver mines... There is scarcely any great American industry that has not had one of this family among its chief promoters. The family has cost the country nothing in pauperism, in crime, in hospitals or asylum service; on the contrary, it represents the highest usefulness. The line still continues to be vigorous, intelligent, enlivening to society. Yet all this achievement came out of a family with no large inherited fortune. All the children's accomplishments were the results of their personal initiative."

This is not to blink at one naughty son and a grandson who were so sensationally shady that the Edwards traits seem to be printed on them in reverse, like the negative of a film. In each case, however, the way the child turned out was the result of exterior circumstances, beyond the control of Sarah Edwards.

Has any other mother contributed more vitality to the leadership of a nation?

How the children turn out is always a reflection on their mother. In the Edwards' case, where the mother had unusual responsibility for managing the household, the children are particularly revealing. Daughters catch their view of what it means to be a woman from their mother's view of her own femininity. The Edwards girls were exceptionally attractive to men, and fortunate in their choice of men to marry. (The talent for choosing the right mate is not one that distinguishes every famous family.) Winship states that "the family has never lost tone through marriage, for its members have chosen men and women of like character and capacity."

Every account of the Edwards home has the same ring. All visitors seem to have been impressed that eleven children managed to be lively and individual as personalities, yet could act courteously with one another and function as a coordinated unit. There may be a key to the many puzzlement's of a parent today in a scrutiny of the way Sarah Edwards helped her children become strong characters.

Her way was not at all permissive. The requirements were completely clear. But she at the same time allowed the children areas of flexibility that were unusual for that day, and she certainly managed to produce a line of remarkable people.

Chapter 15 – Discussion Questions

1. Sarah Edwards said, "… until a child will obey his parents, he can never be brought to obey God." How can this help develop resolve in your heart to not give up training your children to obey?

2. Concerning the Edwards family: "One source of the family stability was the steady, dependable routine of prayers which they had together, before breakfast and again after supper." Do you pray with your wife and with your children daily? Do you pray for them?

3. We may be tempted to dismiss some of the Wesley and Edwards methods as archaic, not possible in today's "progressive" society. What timeless truths can you find in their parenting that will help you to develop godly children like they did?

16
A Servant and his Right Arm

In the last chapter, we looked at two exemplary mothers of times past. But what about today? Are there women working with their families today like those two heroines from the last chapter? I'm convinced that there are many amazing examples all around us of women who are sacrificing and building and working right alongside their husbands. (I can say that because I happen to know many of them personally!)

However, before we get any further down the road, let's take a little detour and take some time to talk about the different roles God has given to husbands and wives. We cannot effectively parent the next generation until we have worked through this high-level issue in our own hearts as men and women and as moms and dads.

Let me share a story with you that I think accurately reflects these differing roles.

Many years ago my wife Neva and I boarded a school bus late one Friday night in Ames, Iowa, to go to a college student conference in Birmingham, Alabama. It was a regional, Christian, student conference.

Neva and I were in one seat and another couple was sitting in the seat right ahead of us. We didn't have any children at the time, but they were expecting a baby. The four of us talked and talked long into the night as we bumped along the road.

Neva and I were pretty new to the church and didn't know a lot of people. This couple, however, impressed us to no end. The husband was continually serving and leading – not just serving his wife but the entire busload of people!

If the bus made a simple gas stop, he ran out to help, checking the oil, finding the restrooms, asking not only his wife whether she needed anything, but my wife, too. As the night wore on, if the spirit of the Christians was getting a little low, he lifted it through his countenance and attitude. If need be, he would lead us all in song. Not only was he serving in this way, but his wife picked up the conversation whenever he took a turn driving as she answered our questions and explained the vision they shared for their lives.

Her quiet dignity and assurance displayed real strength of character in a pretty trying situation. Remember that she was pregnant. If you've never ridden cross-country on an old school bus all night, you don't know what you're missing. Four in the morning reveals the character of a person like no other hour of the day!

Finally, around sun-up, we decided to catch a little sleep. I hadn't thought much about how tired they might be. Neva fell asleep on my shoulder and I soon followed. A little while later, I awoke enough to open one eye and saw that the husband was driving the bus. His wife was quietly lying on the small seat in front of us.

When I awoke again (you don't really sleep too soundly sitting up on a bumpy bus!), I noticed that his turn at driving was over but that he was not on the seat with his wife. Instead, he was curled up on the floor of the bus so that he wouldn't bother his wife, who was sleeping soundly. He awoke before I did to continue his work, in physical service and with his spirit. I determined to follow his example throughout the day.

"The world is sick of little buttoned-up clergymen mumbling canned creeds. It wants real men, men who believe enough to sacrifice for it."

- John Wesley

There was a lot about his lifestyle and discipline that spoke to me during that trip. He demonstrated internal strength and initiative. His wife not only followed, but followed him cheerfully. She was not simply a spectator, but ably played a vital part in his ministry. Her conversation never betrayed any complaints. She seemed to actually be content, although I'm sure the trip was harder on her than any of the rest of us.

I could tell that not only did this husband have an unusual inner motivation, but that he had successfully built it into his wife. I wanted that not only for my own life, but also for my wife and our new marriage, too.

What are we building?

Husband, if you want to know *how* you can more effectively build into your wife, it is important to first establish *what* you should build into her. It's not enough to have a purpose or goal for your wife – it must be the right one! I often talk with men who are regularly spending time alone with their wives on a date, yet are not experiencing all the joy and blessing God intended for their marriage. Frequently they spend more and more time together, yet with seemingly little true progress in their marriage. In my experience, this is because they have a faulty picture of the purpose for their marriage and the direction it should be heading.

You can have a weekly date with your wife, bring her countless flowers (don't get me wrong – flowers are never a bad idea!), have all the routine problems of your household under control and yet still be missing something. That missing piece is God's purpose. If we miss God's purpose, we will consistently miss out on true fulfillment in our marriages.

First and foremost, we husbands have to take the lead and seek to build courage and strength into our wives. Remember that old Cat Stevens song where he was "looking for a hard-headed woman?" Well, so is God.

Our Lord is always searching for a Deborah kind of gal, one who can take action and is not afraid to stand in the gap. He is looking for a woman who will courageously "laugh at the future" (Proverbs 31:25). I am grateful that I have a woman like that in my wife Neva.

Everywhere I go, folks shake my hand and say, "You're married to Neva who writes those great Daylights articles, aren't you?" (Daylights is the daily devotional published by our association of churches.)

I answer "Yes" and wonder if folks might think that Neva is a quiet writer-type and maybe just a little too sweet. When actually her whole family knows her by her well-earned nickname, "Attila the Mom." My own term of endearment for her is – please don't take this wrong – "my sweet battleaxe."

One of the main reasons many men miss out on experiencing God's plan for their marriages is because as husbands they just don't make the effort to build into their wives. Many times guys just won't step up to the plate and take the lead. In fact, studies have shown that the number one problem with our Christian marriages in America today is *a lack of clear leadership from the man.* Why don't more men lead out? I think the major reason is because they don't know where they're going!

Now I'm not talking about all men here. I'm encouraged to know hundreds of men who are not cut from this bolt of cloth – many, many of them within our movement of churches. They are dead serious about winning in every way with their wives and families. They are men of honor and men of action and I am privileged to know them. But by and large, they are a rare commodity.

Our soft society – with its focus on getting off easy – has all but abandoned the idea that sacrifice is something desirable. Yet we cannot overestimate the role that sacrifice has played in our own lives. We have become who we are, in great measure, as a result of the sacrifices that have marked our lives – whether those sacrifices were of our own choosing or from God's sovereign hand.

In the same way, part of God's will and plan for Christian marriages in America is for us to understand and appreciate afresh the value of sacrifice in building and strengthening our lives, in making us the men and women we would never otherwise be.

If we husbands are not building strength and dignity into our wives, we aren't moving in God's direction. It says of that amazing woman in Proverbs 31: "Strength and dignity are her clothing." Just as our clothing is one of the first things people notice about us, so too, God desires that a wife show strength, dignity, and courage as primary traits.

Courage is often demonstrated in our attitude towards sacrifice. In Proverbs 31, the woman "smiles at the future," even when she knows that future involves sacrifice and hard work. She could see it coming, yet she "laughs at the days to come." Our vision of reaching this world with the gospel necessitates sacrifice.

There is no way to avoid sacrifice if we desire to do the job God put us here to do.

For Neva, this sacrifice involves frequent travel, conferences, unexpected delays and problems, evenings when I am out with other men, times when we are apart, and general everyday pressures when I am tied up and she is busy with the work of raising our kids.

As Neva and I give ourselves to the work of the Lord, I always try to discern her spirit and attitude. If her speech is burdened with a recital of all her daily problems, I know that she is losing perspective. I first attempt to work through those daily matters, then encourage and refresh her by reminding her that her sacrifice is having an eternal effect and is helping to advance God's kingdom. And that I appreciate it.

If we try to preserve and protect our marriage selfishly – to shelter our family from sacrifice, to eliminate all trials, to make life easy and comfortable – the Lord promises that we will fail. (Mark 8:34-35). Rather, we must equip and strengthen our wives to face trials with song and joy. (We all, male or female, married or single, should be more concerned about whether our lifestyle is too easy. In our desire to stay inside our comfort zones, we may have lost sight of our "first love" and not even be aware of it.)

For example, I know:

- A couple who gave away their last $5 for the gospel, and they did it with joy and laughter.
- A couple who cut their honeymoon short to bring another couple to a special church conference – and they did it with joy.
- Many couples who have moved out on small teams to help start churches and they, too, did it with joy, not worrying about what it might cost their families. (As a result, God has "given them back" their children as

maturing co-laborers and leaders.)

• Hundreds of women who have chosen to give the very best years of their lives to raising champions for Christ. These are quality women, who could have easily succeeded in a career outside the home, but chose instead to invest in their children. These women demonstrate great faith and true hearts as they "work out their salvation" in their homes on a daily basis!

I once heard a young man state that his wife did not have to demonstrate her faith through staying at home and raising their kids, that there were other ways that she could demonstrate her faith. He's right. There *are* other ways.

However, I know of hundreds of women who have stayed at home and raised a generation for God and shown tested faith in this way every single day. Their kids are now stepping into leadership in universities and colleges and churches and communities across this country. That's because these kids are built out of better quality parts, due primarily to the fact that their moms have made the choices that they have.

And they are still doing it with joy! And they laugh at the future and don't care a whit about the sacrifice. These gals have real courage and tested faith.

Sometimes, the only way to cultivate a joyful response to sacrifice on the part of our wives is to plan times of sacrifice into our marriages to test and develop that quality. Maybe put aside convenience and attend a certain conference, go witnessing on your "date night," or refrain from buying a certain household item in order to have a little extra money to invest in God's kingdom.

Sometimes, the only way to learn is to *do*. Christian marriage manuals that forget this basic principle are a dime a dozen and worth even less. If your idea of prudence is "playing it safe" and "not rocking the boat," then prudence will be like a cancer in your marriage. People spend all kinds of money to go to camps like Outward Bound that deliberately put them in challenging, stressful situations. Why? Because they know deep down that challenge helps build character.

As husbands we must develop our wives' character through planned sacrifice for the gospel and His church and His people. God commands that we build a spirit of joyful, courageous sacrifice into our wives, and we had best start today. If you wait until everything is perfect in your marriage to begin, you will never start.

Often, we fall into this trap of "waiting until things are better" with people we are discipling. We try to resolve all of their hang-ups, problems and fears first. Instead, what we need to do is get them out of the boat! So too, we can't expect to get all the kinks worked out of our marriages first, and then begin to learn to obey and sacrifice. It will never work. On the contrary, if we first obey, we will find that obedience and sacrifice are actually God's tools to teach us how to be joyful and courageous during the storms of life.

As I attempt to build my wife and present her complete in Christ, I continually focus on this theme. At times, my wife and I sit down and consciously plan how we can most effectively reach out to others and live the courageous lifestyle God has called us to live. As we have concentrated on pursuing God's purpose first in the 30 plus years of our marriage, He has given us a rich and fulfilling relationship – and a life that's a dynamic adventure! He has met all of our needs without fail, and has rewarded us far beyond what we began to envision on that bumpy school bus ride so long ago. Everything we have given up to follow Him, He has given back to us "a hundred times over" (Mark 10:28-30). He is faithful and true to His promises – and He will strongly support you, too, husband, as you step out in faith and build into your wife.

Chapter 16 - Discussion Questions

1. Men, how does your lifestyle compare to the husband on the bus? Women, how does your spirit compare to the wife's?

2. *"The number one problem with our Christian marriages in America today, is a lack of clear leadership from the man."* Men, do you know where you are going? Are you "hanging out" with other men who know where they are going?

3. Are you communicating this vision and direction regularly to your wife? Ask your wife if she feels you do.

4. Are you seeking to live a life of sacrifice or a life of ease and comfort? Men, how will you grow, and help your wife to grow, in inner strength as you give your life for the cause of Christ?

17
Two Job Descriptions from God

The following are two very clear and very biblical job descriptions – one for the Christian husband/father and one for the Christian wife/mother. They are not easy, nor are they trite. Fulfilling these roles that God has outlined for men and women, requires our very best effort – plus the grace, strength and support that only God can provide!

We can not effectively parent apart from understanding and embracing these roles. These job descriptions were first penned by Terry Box, a friend and fellow dad.

Mature Leadership in the Home: A Husband's Role

A man is directed by God to take responsibility for the leadership, provision and protection of his wife and children (Ephesians 5:25-31, 1 Timothy 5:8). Although his wife works along side him in managing a home and raising a family, the burden does not fall on her. It rests on him.

A man is responsible for the welfare of his family, over and above his personal needs. He displays strength as he takes the lead in protecting his family (Job 29:11-17). He is uniquely created by God for this responsibility (Genesis 1:27-28). This sense of ownership and leadership is a natural and mature expression of his manhood. His leadership reveals itself in the strength to serve and to sacrifice for the good of his family (Matthew 20:26-28). He acts as a servant of Christ. He does not assume superiority, but values the strengths of his wife (1 Peter 3:7). He will take into account her ideas and may often adopt them.

He does not have to initiate every action in the home, but feels the responsibility to provide a general "game plan" for family activities, plans and decisions (1 Timothy 3:4). A mature man will accept the burden of the "final say" whenever necessary. He embraces this responsibility, yet because of awareness of his own limitations, he does not presume to think that he always knows what is best. He should seek counsel, he will always pray, but he must "make the call" (Proverbs 19:20-21, 1 Peter 5:5).

After he and his wife have agreed together on the particulars of training the children, he does not sit idly by and let his wife keep law and order in the home (Proverbs 22:6, Proverbs 29:17). A mature husband will take the lead in training and disciplining the children when there is a need for correction.

He realizes that his call to leadership is also a call to repentance and humility. He is aware of the potential abuse of his leadership. He is aware of the concerns of his wife, who is called to follow him. He is aware of his own weaknesses and their effect on his family.

He will be a man of prayer and a man of God's Word – more given to planning, more thoughtful and more intentional in his actions, less carried along by the mood of the moment (Proverbs 3:6, Proverbs 12:24, Proverbs 21:5, Proverbs 24:3-6). He will be more disciplined and ordered, strong and sensitive, and take proper initiative to discuss and meet family needs.

He will "lay down his life" (as Christ did) every day for his family. And if necessary, he will freely give up his own physical life in the defense and protection of his loved ones.

This is the nature of mature, biblical leadership. This description may seem to be beyond a man's ability. Yet it is the biblical standard and must be the standard to which he aspires. A man will not be able to always perfectly lead, but with the help of God he will do his best.

A wife's inclination to follow him is hurt by poor leadership on the part of her husband. Trust can be damaged. A mature man will seek to make it easy for his wife to follow and respect him. However, a woman's submission is not dependent upon the perfection of her husband's leadership. Both must lead and follow without reservation. Her respectful following helps his leadership and his benevolent leadership helps her to follow.

A mature man makes it easy for his wife to follow him.

Mature Submission in the Home: A Wife's Role

A mature woman has the desire to yield to her husband and an inclination to follow his leadership.

She will affirm her husband's calling to leadership and is happy to receive his loving care, strength, provision and protection (Ephesians 5:22-24, 1 Peter 3:1-7). She feels herself enhanced and honored by his servant-leadership. A mature wife is able to nurture her husband's strengths and complement his leadership. Her insights and character make her husband stronger and wiser, and make their relationship richer (Genesis 2:18).

She understands and knows that her husband is not superior and that she is not inferior. She knows that man and woman are different, as made by our Creator. He is weaker in some ways and she is weaker in some ways. He is stronger in some ways and she is stronger in some ways. She is not bothered by this, but is glad to support him and follow his initiative.

A mature wife knows how to bring her ideas to a situation in a way that honors her husband's leadership and does not offend his masculinity (Proverbs 16:21-24, Proverbs 19:13, Proverbs 25:24).

She understands that he needs her support and her contribution to the home and to their relationship (Proverbs 31:10-31). She is fully able to step in with appropriate initiatives of her own to handle the many activities in and around the home and family.

Biblical submission does not mean yielding and following at all costs. Significant abuse or immorality by a man can create an exception. As a woman seeks to follow Christ she may find herself in a position where she cannot follow her husband. *It must be mentioned that because of sin, no submission of one human being to another is absolute.* Christ is the only supreme authority. If her husband chronically refuses to lead, a situation may be present for her to take certain initiatives, independently of him. But in either case – a significant sin or no leadership – she will conduct herself in a way that shows by her attitude and behavior that she does not like filling in for him or resisting him, and that she longs for him to pursue righteousness.

Most women do not find this to be their situation. Imperfections and normal grievances are to be resolved, not turned into reasons to withhold submission. A woman is not called to try and evaluate the quality of her husband's leadership and then measure out her submission accordingly. Likewise, the husband is not to measure out his leadership according to how he evaluates her respect for him and her inclination to follow. We are to lead and to follow as God directs us. The rare exceptions are just that – rare exceptions.

A mature woman has an inner strength. She is tranquil, confident, and self-controlled. She can trust God and does not fear (1 Peter 3:4). This enables her to relate to her husband in ways that respect him and draw the best out of him. Her conduct will enrich their relationship and allow her to find greater joy and fulfillment in that relationship.

This is the nature of mature, biblical submission. This description may seem to be beyond a woman's ability or leave her in a wrongfully vulnerable position. Yet it is the biblical standard and must be the standard to which she aspires. God will honor and protect her. A man's desire to lead and care for his wife can be hurt by her refusal to follow. The care and honor she would have received from his mature leadership would be threatened by her resistance to submission. She would miss a great blessing.

A mature woman makes it easy for her husband to care for her.

Chapter 17 – Discussion Questions

1. Men, what are three aspects of this Biblical job description that inspires you?

2. Men, which portion of the list is most challenging?

3. Women, what are three aspects of this Biblical job description that inspires you?

4. Women, which portion of the list is most challenging?

18
The God Factor:
Praying for your
children

"I have never been deeply concerned and prayed about anything, but that it did not come. No matter how long the time, somehow, in some shape, it came."

- Adonirum Judson

Even if we do everything right – or at least the best we know how – God will still examine our hearts. Even when we have tried to be faithful in training our children towards obedience and cheerfulness, He will still evaluate us. God will look into our hearts as parents and ask us a few penetrating questions.

Here are a couple of questions that He has asked me.

- Are you trusting in your methods or in Me, Rick?
- With all your training, are you *praying* for your kids?

Our Lord wants to see if we are trusting in Him. Obviously God believes in godly discipline. He was the One Who first taught us all these things in His Word. But in the midst of all of our training He still asks, "In Whom are you trusting?"

With this in mind, let's talk about prayer.

"But they were startled and frightened... And He said to them, 'Why are you troubled, and why do doubts arise in your hearts?'"

- Luke 24:37-38

Awhile back I was in the Smithsonian National Museum of Art and an intriguing painting caught my attention. I don't know who the painter was, but the painting was one of those grand, lush, romantic landscapes that were so popular at the beginning of the last century.

In the painting was a wide river lined on both sides with cottonwoods. There was a violent summer thunderstorm going on. The wind was viciously whipping the trees back and forth. Black clouds were boiling down over the river, with jagged lightning forking the sky. And in the center of the river, buffeted by the howling wind and waves, was a cattle barge.

The boat was rocking violently as the bellowing cattle crashed from side to side, their big horns slicing the air. I was gripped by the look of panic in their eyes and the heroic efforts of the bargemen. Any minute you thought the whole thing was going to tip over and everything would be lost – the cattle, the barge, maybe even those men.

But it was the title that made me smile and then stop and think. Despite all of the turmoil, excitement and danger on the canvas, the painter titled it, "Just Changing Pastures."

Instead of calling it "Caught in the Storm" or "Dangers on the River," the painter chose to give us a broader perspective.

We need a similar perspective on life. God is encouraging this kind of larger outlook in Psalm 37:7 when He says, "Rest in the Lord." Rest in the Lord – no matter what we are up against. No matter how severe our present trials may seem, they usually just involve marriage or kids or jobs, etc. And people have been getting married, raising kids and going to work since the beginning of time.

Why not relax and ease up? Life isn't really that bad. Why not "rest in the Lord?" No matter what it is that we are going through, we're really only "just changing pastures." God has the whole of our lives under control. If we believe this, how are we demonstrating our trust in Him?

Are we reading His Book and trusting in what we are reading? Are we praying like we ought to – for our lives, our marriages and our children? Do we really believe that He hears us?

"Behold, the Lord's hand it not so short that it cannot save, neither is His ear so dull, that it cannot hear."

- Isaiah 59:1

Let me tell you a true story that happened to me, many summers ago. It illustrates just how clearly God hears us.

It was the middle of July, very hot and very dry, and it was time to vaccinate and brand the calves. So one morning, with some of us in pickups and most of us on horseback, we drove 600 cows – with their 600 calves trailing at their sides – down towards the working corrals near the watering tanks at the bottom of a section of pasture land.

We worked all day corralling and sorting out those 600 black cows and leaving their 600 calves separated in another pen. It was the dustiest, noisiest scene of confusion I've ever witnessed. We finished sorting by late afternoon and left the calves penned up, planning to start working on them at sunup the following day.

Very early the next morning, as I drove up to the ranch's main buildings and got out of my car, I initially felt and then heard what sounded like a 747 jet airplane taking off two miles away down at those corrals. I finally figured out that the roar was the sound of those cows and their calves raising holy heck.

We got our branding irons, vaccination gear and the rest of our equipment loaded into the pickups and took off for those pens. The closer we got, the louder the sound became, until we crossed the last hill and looked down toward the corral. With my head stuck out the window, I could almost feel the impact of so much concentrated sound hitting my face.

There was a heavy dew that morning, but what you saw driving down towards the center of the valley was a large, brown cloud of dust, hanging kind of low. That dust was being kicked up by 2400 tiny hooves inside the corral and 2400 mamma hooves outside the pen. Every single calf and every single cow was bawling and bellowing for breakfast.

They were upset and angry and the full 1200 of those black creatures were complaining all at once. The dirt in and around those pens was beaten a full inch deep, as fine as flour.

They must have been circling all night long, hour after hour. The calves were hungry. The mamas with swollen udders were upset. And all of them were very vocal about it.

We worked all day in the choking dust and sun, unable to hear ourselves think, much less hear each other speak. At *first I felt that I had to open my mouth just to release the pressure on my eardrums.*

But one by one we hustled through those calves and processed each of them – ear-tagged them, branded them, vaccinated them – and then turned them loose.

And here is the amazing part: In all that heat and noise and dust and racket, as we turned each calf loose and pushed him through the corral's gate out to where the cows were, in all that noise the cow and the calf could actually hear each other!

As that calf let out a quick calf bawl, out of those 600 black cows the "mama" would come running up at a gallop to find and nuzzle her calf. She would laser right in on him based solely on the sound of his cry. Then she would immediately lead her "baby" off over the hills away from all that pandemonium.

Each time we let one go, it seemed that the cow could hear her calf just as clearly as if the two of them were all alone and there was not another calf on the face of the earth.

If the Lord could create that kind of hearing in a cow, don't you think He can hear us when we pray to Him during a typical, noisy day? When we beseech Him to move in our children's lives and to teach us how to parent them? Of course He hears us!

Taking it to heart

But sometimes it's *our* hearing that's not so great.

Prayer is something we Christians hear about often. Unfortunately, that's probably because we *need* to hear about it often. For we often fail to take what we hear to heart.

I've been a Christian for many years. For a few of those years I was not convinced of the vital importance of prayer. Oh, I prayed, but it certainly wasn't the top priority in my life.

I distinctly remember hearing a mature Christian brother speak about the importance of prayer many years ago. I listened and knew that what he was saying was right. I knew I needed to change my prayer habits (actually, my lack of prayer habits). I took careful notes. Yet I didn't take it to heart.

Oh, I prayed – but I didn't pray as I should. Prayer wasn't a vital part of my life. It wasn't in my blood, in my spirit. It wasn't driven deep into my heart, into my life. It wasn't gripping me! I suffered from my lack of prayer for many years.

God had to personally convince me of how vital prayer is, of how crucial it is to hearing from Him through His Word. I believe that if a man has trouble getting into the Word – and getting something from God out of it – it's probably because he's not praying as he ought. When I really began letting God grip my heart in prayer, His Word just came alive in my life!

Removing the roadblocks

None of us wants to have a weak, anemic relationship with God. We want to know Him intimately and experience His power in our daily lives. We don't want anything to block our life-giving connection with our Lord. So let's briefly take a look at a few things that can hinder prayer in our lives as fathers and as men who want to make a difference:

- **Sin** – One thing that hinders God from working through our prayers is sin. Psalm 66:18 says, "If I regard iniquity in my heart, Thou wilt not hear me." This verse doesn't mean that we need to go looking for sin in our hearts, but rather that if God has brought an area of sin to our attention, we need to deal with it.

- **Self-sufficiency** – A second thing that can hinder prayer is a self-sufficient attitude – for example, an attitude that says "I don't need to talk to God about this; I can handle it myself." Relying on God and His wisdom in all things is a good habit to get into, men. Develop this habit, no matter how strong you may think you are.

- **Distrust** – A third hindrance to prayer is distrust. We pray, yet we don't really trust. We don't believe God will work in our particular circumstance. And, of course, without faith He doesn't. When He doesn't work and help us, we tend to eventually stop asking Him to. It's a vicious circle.

  Without faith, it is impossible to please God. If we have believed in Him for our salvation, certainly we can believe in Him for our circumstances. We need to recognize distrust for what it really is – plain old sin. It's the attitude of unbelievers, of the lost. We fathers especially should be ones who are leading out in prayer in front of our wives and our families. It reveals to them that we too are also trustingly submitting to our Lord.

Becoming effective

Okay, so suppose we get these hindrances to prayer out of the way and now we're ready to pray. Just how should we go about it? What should the character and spirit of our prayers be? What should they feel like? What is good praying? Let's look at some simple steps that can help instill effective prayer in our lives.

- **Use your head** – First, be lspecific and think about what you're asking God for. Paul told the Corinthians, "I shall pray with the spirit and I shall pray with the mind also" (I Cor. 14:15). This kind of prayer is hard work. James in his epistle says that the energetic, fervent prayer of a righteous man is able to accomplish much. You get the idea that this is ordered, intentional prayer.

- **Schedule it in** – Secondly, scheduling an ordered time of prayer is vital. Turning to God throughout the day is important, but in my experience, spontaneous prayer is the fruit of an ordered time of prayer – not the other way around.

- **Keep a prayer list** – Thirdly, keeping a prayer list can also help you be more specific in prayer. It causes you to order your prayers and think and beseech and persevere. It'll also help build your faith when God answers those same prayers. You can't judge the effect of prayer after just one day. But if you keep a prayer list every day – jotting down just a brief thought as you're praying – at the end of a month you will see answers. Commit to working on this habit for one month, and at the end of that month I guarantee your faith will be stronger.

Why? Because we often forget when He answers prayer. You can go back through a prayer list and see that prayer that you offered earlier and forgot. But God didn't forget; He answered it!

Initially when I pray, the request side of the page always seems longer, while the receiving side of the page is somewhat short. However, as I go back and review my written record, I begin to see more and more answers.

This causes my faith to grow and it will cause your faith to grow, too.

- **Be intense about it** – A fourth thing that helps our prayer lives is intensity. If we value prayer, if our heart is in it, we'll be intense. If lack of prayer has been a chronic problem in your Christian life over the past months or years, it can change. It can change right this minute if you want it to. Ask God to change your attitude about prayer and begin to talk to your Lord about it right now.

  Be intense! You can't pray intensely and stay the same. Prayer changes us. It should always change us, men. If it doesn't change us, something is wrong.

  When I speak of being intense, I'm not talking about cheap emotion. Too many Christians are involved in this kind of shallowness. They show up at prayer meetings and automatically the tears flow. I wonder if these Christians pray like that in private? After all, what you pray in private is all that is genuine. That's why I believe intensity in prayer begins alone. Pharisees can pray intensely in public without praying intensely in private, but Christians can't. We must be devoted to our quiet, secret, closet times with the Lord. Of course it's great to join together in prayer as a church, but our united public prayer is only as effective as our private individual prayer.

- **Spend time at it** – The last thing that helps prayer develop in our lives is to make sure we actually spend time at it! I don't want you to be discouraged by a false standard of trying to spend many hours in prayer. For most of us, I would guess that 15 minutes a day spent in prayer would be progress. I don't say this to shame us, but simply to encourage prayer. Moms and dads, we would be greatly blessed if we prayed for just a quarter of an hour every day.

I'm not talking about reading the Word or singing or listening to Christian music, I'm talking about spending fifteen minutes in solid prayer. Just fifteen minutes a day would be helpful and encouraging. Remember, it's step by step that we inherit the land.

Getting in shape

The legendary Vince Lombardi, who coached the Green Bay Packers during their early glory years, lived and breathed football – and football practice, in particular. He put his players through extremely rigorous training. So hard, in fact, was their training that many of them looked forward to the day of the game for relief. Lombardi knew that winning came only through conditioning, and I believe the same is true for Christians. Christians are conditioned by God and strengthened in their souls through prayer. Without prayer, we're simply not in shape to take the victory God wants for us.

So what kind of shape are you in? Are you receiving fresh strength and power from God daily? Are things sort of hit-and-miss? Somewhere in between? I encourage you to evaluate your own condition right now. Ask God how you're doing. And then determine in your heart to obey Him in whatever He reveals to you.

As John Wesley said, "God does nothing but in answer to prayer." God Himself tells us in Jeremiah 33:3, "Call unto Me, and I will answer you and show you great and mighty things that you have not seen." This excites me, men. Our prayers move God to action!

So don't give up, parents. Keep your eyes on God by thinking about your prayers. Have an ordered time of prayer and keep a prayer list. Show intensity in your prayer life and spend time at it. Ask and keep on asking, for "he who asks, receives!"

What to pray for

Are you at a loss as to what to pray for? You might pray the prayer that my wife has prayed for our children for many years: "Lord, I pray that they will always be found out." (always caught, never able to deceive, charm, etc.)

That's a good one, isn't it? Here are a few more. Pray that your children will respect authority. Pray that they will be single-hearted and sold out to Christ. Pray that they will have hearts that repent quickly.

In conclusion, here are seven practical areas that parents can use as guidelines as they pray for their children – one for every day of the week – courtesy of my good friend, John Hopler. (Thanks, John, for your faithful friendship and for faithfully fathering your own clan!)

Seven Days of Prayer for Our Family
(The ABC's)

Sunday – Pray that we would be **A**stonished by God's work in our family.

Monday – Pray that our children would do **B**etter works than their parents.

Tuesday – Pray that our kids would have <u>C</u>hrist-like values and character.

Wednesday – Pray that all of our <u>D</u>escendants would be saved.

Thursday – Pray that our children would become <u>E</u>xcellent spouses and find good mates.

Friday – Pray that our family would be <u>F</u>ree from moral impurity.

Saturday – Pray that we'd be a <u>G</u>reat Commission family.

Chapter 18 - Discussion Questions

1. Are you praying, or are you "going through the motions?"

2. Three hindrances to prayer are sin, self-sufficiency, and distrust. Are any of these hindering you right now?

3. How do you want to increase your faith and time in prayer? Ask someone to join with you in accountability for prayer, someone who has the faithfulness to regularly ask you how your prayer life is, and who has the courage to urge you to keep pressing on.

19
Of Fence Posts and Young Men

"A boy by the age of three years senses that his destiny is to be a man, so he watches his father particularly – his interests, manner, speech, pleasures, his attitude towards work... "

- Michael B. Rothenberg

Did you know that kids – especially boys – just really want to be with their dads?

The surprising truth about kids is that they really want to be close to their parents. In 1996, <u>Careers and Colleges</u> magazine conducted a survey of teenagers and asked them to name the number one person they admired. Among the males, 73% picked their fathers above everyone else!

John Wooden, the legendary basketball coach from UCLA shares the following in his autobiography, <u>They Call Me Coach</u>. He talks about the influence his father had on his life. Coach

Wooden is legendary mainly for the character he has shown over the years and here he states that he learned it from his dad.

"Actually, my father has had a profound influence on my life. Both my philosophy of life and of coaching came largely from him. Even as a small boy I always had great respect for him because I knew he would always be fair with me and had my best interests at heart. And I soon learned that if he couldn't say something good about another person, he wouldn't say anything at all, a philosophy I've tried to follow.

A truly gentle man, dad read the Bible daily; he wanted us to read it, and we did. That is probably why I keep a copy on my desk today. It's not a decoration, but is well marked and read. The fact that I never heard dad swear, along with the incident in the barn, surely accounts for the fact that even today when I get mad, the strongest thing I can say is "goodness gracious sakes alive.""

Each father needs to take advantage of this built-in tendency to hero-worship and develop a strong relationship with his children. With that in mind, here are several stories that deal with learning life lessons that I hope will inspire you like they have me.

I ran across the first one while I was thumbing through an old agriculture magazine recently. A farmer was recounting his memories of working with his own father as he was growing up, in particular his memories about helping his dad build fence and dig those countless postholes. Before I share the concluding quote with you, I need to set the stage a little:

The sun was always hot. Building fence was a lot of hard work and he seemed to start sweating as soon as he picked up the shovel.

As a younger boy, he remembered helping his dad and watching him dig the postholes and tamp the dirt. He thought that the holes were deep enough to reach to China before his dad would ever quit digging! And then setting the fence posts, tamping them, packing the dirt around them, always ended with a certain sound.

He explained how his dad would tamp the dirt in the hole with a steel bar and that it would finally "ring" when the dirt was solidly packed.

The last test, however came after the post was tamped in.

To check that it was set right, his dad would slap it hard. If it was set properly and solidly, it would vibrate and "bite you back."

The author had taken a trip home and went up to a fence post that he had helped set with his father some forty years earlier. He slapped it hard.

He concluded his article with these words:

"I slapped it. Maybe it was my chance to get even for all of the sweat and aching muscles that corner post had caused. And maybe a little leftover resentment towards dad. But still it bit me back. The vibration from my slap seemed to run from my hand, up my arm, and all the way down to my boots. That old post was still as solidly set as the day it was first tamped down."

We don't seem to set them as solid as that anymore, fence posts or young men.

How true and how sad. We as a nation are not that concerned about our sons. Even in our churches, we're often not that concerned.

Many of us are not spending the time and "doing it right" in raising these boys.

Thank God that there are a few fathers out there who are looking down the road and doing it right, setting those young "posts" solidly in the ground.

When we do it right, our sons will "ring true" for fifty years and more.

The next illustration, taken from Dr. James Dobson's newsletter, is a personal story about the youth of Dr. John Corts, former president of the Billy Graham Evangelistic Association. He is "John" in the story:

When he was 16 years of age, he and his younger cousins went to visit his grandfather's farm. They couldn't wait to get there and go out into the fields. They wanted to pitch hay and ride on the tractor. It sounded like so much fun.

But the grandfather was reluctant to let them go. They whined and begged until he finally said to John, "You are the oldest. You can take the kids to the field if you promise not to bring them back early. You must keep them out there until the end of the day."

John said, "I will do that, Grandfather."

So they all got on the hay wagon and the tractor pulled them out to the field.

Very quickly, the kids got tired, and they started complaining. It was hot and sticky, and they were miserable. They began asking to go back to the house.

But John said, "No, Grandfather told me to keep you out here."

At lunchtime, they were exhausted, and most of his cousins were angry. It was very hot. The hay was down their backs, and it itched. They wanted to go back.

But again John said, "No, Grandfather told me to keep you here."

At about 3:00 in the afternoon, a big black storm cloud

came over, and the kids got kinda scared. Some were crying.
"Please!" they begged. "Let's go home."
Still, the answer remained "No."
About 5:00 in the afternoon, John said, "All right, it's
time to quit."
He got them all on the hay wagon, and they went back to
the house. After they had had their baths and been given
something to eat, they rested for a while. Grandfather praised
them warmly for the work they had done. Then, the cousins
all became very proud of themselves.
That's when Grandfather told John why he wanted them
to stay in the field.
He said, "This farm has been successful through the years
for one reason. We have stayed in the field when we felt like
coming in. We did what needed to be done even when we
wanted to quit. That is why I wanted the kids to have the
satisfaction of staying with something through the day."

Dr. Dobson goes on to say, "God has called us to stay in the
field, to the end of the day, and we will do that for as long as we
have breath in our bodies. If we persevere to the end, we will
hear those wonderful words of the Father, 'Well done, thou good
and faithful servant.'"

We've been talking about learning life's lessons through
everyday things. In the first story we talked about building fence
as a picture of building boys. Then we read about putting up hay
and the lessons that young men can learn when they stick it out.
Now let's talk about young men and playing sports and the life
lessons to be learned there. We could talk about any sport and
the lessons it can teach a young man, but I want to talk about
wrestling. (Because I am writing this book!)

The apostle Paul wrote, "For we wrestle not against flesh and blood, but against principalities, against powers, against the rulers of the darkness of this world, against spiritual wickedness in high places" (Ephesians 6:12).

When you think about it, we are all wrestlers in one way or another. With that in mind, I'd like to relate a few stories lifted from the pages of our lives these last two years as we have cheered on a young wrestler who has become a young man in the process, our son Mike. It is part letter, part sportscast, with a good dose of parental musings thrown in for good measure – more like a long conversation than anything else. So follow along...

Dear Wrestling Fans,

I have a few minutes this morning and decided I'd share a few things that have been running through my mind this last 24 hours. I have been thinking about my boy Mike.

"The righteous face many troubles, but the LORD rescues them from each and every one."

- Psalm 34:19

Obviously I am a little saddened that he is so sick, here right before he wrestles at the biggest tournament of his young life. He is one sick kid with a bad case of the flu.

But here is what I have been chewing on...

Two years ago after Mike finished eighth grade with a state championship (they have a "little league" state wrestling tournament here in Colorado), we went to a dual meet on a Saturday afternoon, "just for grins."

Halfway through the match, behind 8 to 0, Mike felt his knee give way. He heard and felt a pop and we found out later that he had torn the meniscus cartilage. Immediately after this knee injury there was a "blood" time-out. (He bleeds a lot. He seems to put his head where he shouldn't.) I was standing at the edge of the mat and heard Mike tell his coach, "Something's wrong with my knee, Coach." But he shook it off and walked around the mat and continued to wrestle.

He won at the end of the third period with just seconds to go. After the match, the coach turned to me and said, "You have a tough kid there, Dad."

We took Mike to the surgeon, where the doctor first "scoped" his knee and then later in the operation, wound up cutting it open because it was worse than he thought. Mike was on crutches for three months. Since he couldn't participate in any phys ed classes at school, he asked the coach if he would just leave him locked in the weight room on the stationary bike during PE.

The coach agreed and Mike asked if he could also have one of his teammates locked in the room with him. Well, that boy prayed to receive Christ with Mike at the end of the hour! Two weeks later another teammate asked to ride on the stationary bike in the weight room alongside Mike, and he also prayed with my boy at the end of the hour to accept Christ!

That was what encouraged me most about his eighth grade year.

Last year, he was the only freshman to make the varsity squad. He wrestled at 171 pounds. Here are two stories that encouraged me from Mike's freshman year.

That year our team sent 7 seniors to State, a solid, tough team. These upperclassmen were all very good wrestlers, yet towards the end of the year, a number of them came up to my freshman and asked him what he prayed about before his matches. (They had seen him behind the bleachers down on a knee for a minute, right before he went out on the mat.)

Mike said, "You guys don't want to hear my prayer."

But they insisted.

So he told them, "I pray that you guys would be proud of me. I pray that Dad would be proud of me and that Coach would be proud of me. I pray that I would wrestle to the best of my ability and I pray that I will not be injured." (He got beat up all year long, but he just did not want to have another knee injury.)

After hearing that, several of the seniors said, "We love you Whitney. You're alright." Several of those seniors singled me out at the end of the year and told me how much they appreciated Mike's spirit. "He doesn't quit, Mr. Whitney," they said.

The second story that encouraged me from Mike's freshman year was one I heard – rather belatedly – for the first time just the other day. At school one of the upper classmen on that wrestling squad told Mike's older sister what had happened during a team trip to a tournament over the Christmas break last year. Mike had never shared it with any of us.

The wrestling team had taken off on this three-day trip to a big tournament in western Colorado. On the last night, the whole team decided to walk down to a hamburger shop to get something to eat. (the coaches were at the motel.) As the team walked back to the hotel, they saw a gas station and decided to initiate the only freshman in the group. (my son.)

"Whitney, here's enough money. We want you to go in that gas station and buy a Playboy magazine."

At this point my boy did the only thing he could think of. He refused and took off running down the road, away from the gas pumps!

The seniors were scared then! They were responsible for him and for the whole team.

He had gotten a block or two ahead and they were running after him and started shouting, "Whitney, hold up. You don't need to do it."

He didn't compromise. They didn't buy the magazine after all.

That year he wound up with a record of 26-10. He didn't get through Regionals with all those good senior wrestlers, but he gained their respect and also, I heard, their affection.

"You don't raise heroes, you raise sons. And if you treat them like sons, they'll turn out to be heroes, even if it's just in your own eyes."

- Walter M. Schirra, Sr.

This year as a sophomore he is wrestling at 189 and is 28-3.

He has been throwing up for the last 24 hours, but he is determined to wrestle tonight in the opening round of our state tournament at the Pepsi Center in downtown Denver.

I shared this verse with him last night.

"The human spirit can endure a sick body, but who can bear it if the spirit is crushed?"

-Proverbs 18:14

He said, "I'm ready, Dad. Whether I'm even sick on the mat, I'm going!"

What has encouraged me the most this year happened just

last week. I heard this story from one of the other wrestlers.

At Regionals, every wrestler in Colorado has a chance to qualify for State. And whether you win or lose in the opening rounds, you still have a chance to go to State if you wrestle well in consolation. After the first night's matches though, it gets pretty intense.

Mike and several other boys were still wrestling in the winner's bracket and the rest of the squad was still alive on the consolation side. The boys were all very serious, kind of afraid, pretty nervous. Many of them were upperclassmen and this was their last chance to qualify for State.

On Saturday morning on the last day of the tournament, the team all gathered together and out of the blue some of the seniors asked Mike if he would pray for them all.

They said, "We'll just listen, if you will pray for us, Mike."

So he did.

I was obviously encouraged that they would turn to a sophomore when the going got tense and tough.

"Your goodness is so great! You have stored up great blessings for those who honor you. You have done so much for those who come to you for protection, blessing them before the watching world."

- Psalm 31:19

Anyway, those are just a couple thoughts that have come to mind today as I watch him – sick as a dog, but determined.

Brothers, we really are raising a whole different caliber of kids.

They truly are all champions. Or at least they all can be.

Don't ever forget the incredible potential of the kind of young people we have sitting at our dinner tables every night! I'll let you know if he gets through the first round. Either way he has blessed my heart already.

Keep pressing,
Rick

(Two days later...)

He made it through the first round – and the second round, where he pinned an undefeated senior! Then Mike lost in the semifinals to the eventual state champion. But came back strong in the consolation bracket and wound up third at State! (All of the top six placers at State at 189 lbs. were seniors, except for my boy.) We are very proud. He finished the year 32 and 4. He loves wrestling!

(One year later...)

Dear Brothers,
Well, Mike made it through Regionals and is on to State this week!
His first match is Thursday night. His record is 30 and 4. He won a few tournaments earlier in the year and was second in a few big tournaments. He is now a junior.
But this is State!
You might offer a prayer that his knee would hold up. A couple of years ago he had one knee first "scoped" and then operated on. But this is his other knee.
He wrenched it pretty badly last week and had to wear a

brace at the Regionals over the weekend in Grand Junction. The brace slows him down some, but maybe he won't need it for State.

I have included two more pieces of writing for you to chew on. The first deals with wrestling. Since the Apostle Paul was a wrestler – and since we are all wrestlers, as Paul describes it – I thought you guys would appreciate this poster that Mike has on his wall at home:

I wrestle.
Not simply with my opponent.

I wrestle with demons of doubt.
With my past failures.
With my exhaustion.
With my injuries.
With my anonymity.

With that unrelenting voice that tells me to stop.
But I am a wrestler.
And one thing will always be certain.
I will not quit.

This second piece deals with two of my favorite characters from the Old West. (When we were in Grand Junction at Regionals last weekend, I felt like I had stepped into a John Wayne movie set. Colorado's "western slope," with its towering buttes and mesas, is just how I picture the Old West.)

I've been encouraging Mike recently with the following portion of the book <u>Dead Man's Walk</u> by Larry McMurtry. Mike is a pretty good wrestler, not a bad technician. But I have been telling him that what is called for now is a certain kind of "wildness."

He knows this is true.

(Let me set the stage for you. The year is around 1840 and the place is the wastelands of west Texas. Our heroes, Gus and Call, are very young men, boys really, just recently recruited into the Texas Rangers. Comanches are decimating their ranks. Their job is to escort a British Lady, who has been at a Spanish mission, across these wild lands to eastern Texas and civilization. Here is the passage and the lesson.)

"In the vastness of the desert each reduction of the group made them realize how small they were, how puny, in relation to the space they were traveling through.

"We're back where it's wild again," Call said.

Lady Carey happened to overhear the remark – she drew rein for a moment, looking toward a faint outline of mountains in the east.

"Yes, it's wild, isn't it," she said. "It's like a smell. I smelled it in Africa and now I smell it here."

"It means we have to be careful," Call said.

Lady Carey looked again at the distant mountains. "Quite the contrary, Corporal Call," she said. "It means we have to be wild, like the wild men."

She turned her head toward him and sat watching him for a moment.

Call couldn't see her eyes through the several dark veils, but he knew she was watching him. Although she had been always polite, Call felt nervous, knowing that her hidden eyes were fixed on him.

"Are you wild enough, Corporal Call?" Lady Carey asked. "I have a feeling you are."

"I guess we'll see," Call said."

When I think of the kind of wildness mentioned here, I think of zeal. God has called us all to practice this special kind of wildness. (And so we will be wildly screaming our heads off Thursday night at the Pepsi Center!)

The point is, boys need to be wild at times. Not the kind of foolish wildness that the world glorifies, but a good wildness that paves the way for heroic actions. A wildness that is full of courage and risk.

The theme of this chapter is young men and their fathers and the kind of spirit we need to be imparting to these boys while they're still young. The Bible clearly states that at some point the sons will replace the fathers. Our sons will grow up and step forward to serve God right alongside their dads. And then, Lord willing, they will go far beyond us.

Here is a true story of how another committed dad I know accomplished this with his own son.

Many years ago, one of the first dads to join up with our new church in Gainesville, Florida, was a dear man named Walt Nemecek. He was a good man, a guy who became a very good friend to me. At the time I met him, Walt's little boy had just come out of chemotherapy for the treatment of leukemia. Because of it, the little boy only had a few wisps of blonde hair here and there; otherwise he was almost totally bald. He was a sight at that time, even though he was very cute. And we were, of course, concerned for him and for the family.

Many years went by. I hadn't seen Walt's little boy for a long time, but then out of the blue I had the chance to see him at a prayer meeting in the Southeast. That "boy" is now over 25 years old. He is married and has kids of his own. He is taller than I am and has teamed up with another good man to plant a new church. A full head of dark hair has replaced the golden wisps I remember.

(I told him that he is the only guy I know who has *gained* hair as the years go by!)

I kept thinking of Walt as I prayed with his son. I am sure that Walt is very proud of his grown boy.

"In place of the fathers shall be your sons."

I remember the big heart Walt has always shown. I haven't had the opportunity to work with his son, but if he has planted a church this year, then he too must have his father's big heart. (And he'll *need* his father's big heart.)

I was reminded of Walt's openness and genuineness as I prayed with his boy. Walt is a "hale and hearty" kind of guy and a truly friendly man. He is comfortable to be around. So is his boy. Easy smile, friendly face. Just like his dad.

Every Christian parent I have ever known desires that his children go on in the faith. We are incredibly happy when we know that our offspring have wholeheartedly embraced our Christian faith and are giving it their very lives. Yet I believe that the only way we will see this accomplished is through the careful cultivation of our own hearts as fathers.

Our children know us. They can read our hearts. We cannot guide them where we have not gone. We cannot give them what we do not have. Maybe the first half of that favorite verse should read, *"I will give you my heart first*, now give me your heart, my son."

Walt Nemecek's heart can be read by all as they listen to his son Vashi. Walt's love for people is now a part of his boy's way of life.

And now Walt's heart can be seen through two witnesses.

I'd like to conclude with a very famous poem that I believe
captures the spirit of what we're trying to instill into our sons.

"*If*"   - by Rudyard Kipling

If you can keep your head when all about you
Are losing theirs and blaming it on you;
If you can trust yourself when all men doubt you,
But make allowance for their doubting too:
If you can wait and not be tired by waiting,
Or being lied about, don't deal in lies,
Or being hated, don't give way to hating,
And yet don't look too good, nor talk too wise;

If you can dream – and not make dreams your master;
If you can think – and not make thoughts your aim,
If you can meet with Triumph and Disaster
And treat those two impostors just the same:
If you can bear to hear the truth you've spoken
Twisted by knaves to make a trap for fools,
Or watch the things you gave your life to, broken,
And stoop and build them up with worn-out tools;

If you can make one heap of all your winnings
And risk it on one turn of pitch-and-toss,
And lose, and start again at your beginnings,
And never breathe a word about your loss:
If you can force your heart and nerve and sinew
To serve your turn long after they are gone,
And so hold on when there is nothing in you
Except the Will which says to them: "Hold on!"

If you can talk with crowds and keep your virtue,
Or walk with Kings – nor lose the common touch,
If neither foes nor loving friends can hurt you,
If all men count with you, but none too much:
If you can fill the unforgiving minute
With sixty seconds' worth of distance run,
Yours is the Earth and everything that's in it,
And - which is more - you'll be a Man, my son!

Chapter 19 – Discussion Questions

1. *"This farm has been successful through the years for one reason. We have stayed in the field when we felt like coming in. We did what needed to be done even when we wanted to quit. That is why I wanted the kids to have the satisfaction of staying with something through the day."*
How are you training your son in courage and perseverance?

2. Is the example of your life "heroic" in these same areas?

3. *"The point is, boys need to be wild at times. Not the kind of foolish wildness that the world glorifies, but a good wildness that paves the way for heroic actions. A wildness that is full of courage and risk."* What does this wildness look like, in practical terms, for your son?

4. How does this differ from the kind of wildness the world promotes?

5. Have your teenage son read the chapter with you, and then discuss.

20
Leading with our spirit

*"But my righteous one shall live by faith, and if he shrinks
back, my soul has no pleasure in him."*

- Hebrews 10:38

An old Keith Green song goes something like this: "My eyes
are dry, my faith is old, my heart is hard, my prayers are cold."
And then the refrain asks, "What can be done with an old heart
like mine?"

What can be done? What if our hearts are dry, old, hard and
cold?

I once heard someone say something startling on this topic of
apathy, dullness of soul and lukewarmness of spirit. He said, "There
is no great future for any people whose faith has burned out." No
future, if our faith has lost its flame.

We are often comforted when we read in God's Word that
our future is bright with the Lord. But what about those seemingly

hardened, cynical believers we all have contact with? And what about *our* cynical attitudes? Have you ever met a Christian who has seemingly quit? All his glory years are past tense. Everything exciting in his spiritual walk occurred ten years ago.

What about us? Have we quit? Is this our posture?

The Scriptures say, "Without faith it is impossible to please Him." If we shrink back from living on the edge, from believing by faith – He has no delight in us! Now I know that the context of this passage deals primarily with salvation. But I also know that if our faith is not of the *daily, using kind*, we are of all people most pitiful.

There is no way we can train and lead our kids without spirit. Parents have to be invigorated for life.

"I spent twenty years trying to come to term with my doubts. Then one day it dawned on me that I had better come to terms with my faith."

- David Roberts

I'm not sure that I have a lot of answers to this daily battle against ennui, but I know that we must fight it. I know that this fight against opting for security is constant.

I know that many people quietly fall asleep in their Christian walk and are never heard from again.

Did you know that real pearls must be worn often to remain lustrous? If they are stored away for long periods of time, their glow begins to fade. Pearls must have regular contact with human skin to remain attractive. Unused pearls grow dull.

What a perfect illustration for the proper use of our faith! Faith needs to be used, not left on the mantle like some dusty, old trophy.

If our eyes are a little dry, if our prayers are a little cold, one sure remedy is to pray a simple, one-sentence prayer before you have your quiet time. One I use all the time. This prayer is guaranteed to electrify your day. It goes like this:

"Lord, here in your Book. Show me something that I can do this day and I will try my best to do it."
Try it. I dare you.

"If you cannot always get the right explanation for some Scripture, be sure you don't miss the application of it."

- Vance Havner

Awhile back I read the book <u>The Acts of King Arthur and His Noble Knights</u> by John Steinbeck. In the story, later in life Queen Guinevere and King Arthur recognized that both they and their knights were sunk in a kind of funk, a doldrums of the spirit.

To be in a "doldrum" out on the high seas is to experience no wind. The sails are limp. The boat is going nowhere. So too were those knights. They were bored and a little stale.

How do you move out of this kind of spiritual listlessness?

The Queen shared the following with her husband, King Arthur.

They need a quest. It is one thing to make oneself great, but quite another to try to be not small. I think that every man wants to be larger than himself, and that he can be, only if he is part of something immeasurably larger than himself.

The best knight in the world, if he is unchallenged, finds himself shrinking. We must seek a way to declare a great war on little things. We must find a word, a thought, a standard, under which small evils may enlist in a great wrong.

That word, that thought, that standard for the Christian is the Word of God.

And the best cause in the world is to be involved in the most challenging, heroic struggle that God has ever left to men. That struggle is the advancement of God's Kingdom here on earth. The salvation of our families, the building up of His church.

When we are energized with His thoughts, when we are memorizing His Bible and sharing what we are learning with each other, our faith comes alive! When family or friends hear how real our faith is, when it actually affects our speech, it will have a deep impact on them. When they hear how real our Lord is to us, it will touch and influence our kids.

"No Christian can be a pessimist, for Christianity is a symbol of radical optimism."

- G. K. Chesterton

The question we need to be asking ourselves as parents, the question that will help us evaluate how we're doing in influencing our kids for Christ is: Do our kids listen to us gladly?

"And all the people would get up early in the morning to come to Him in the temple to listen to Him."

- Luke 21:38

Jesus was very unusual in how He talked. Not just in what He said, but especially in how He went about saying it. Jesus was so confident in Who He was and in the righteousness of His message, that He could afford to be patient with anyone. He did not feel threatened, because He knew He had the answers. As a result,

His speech rang with a freedom and grace that has never been equaled. The people of His day flocked to hear His words and His thoughts and His wisdom.

I have personally been on a quest to try to imitate that quality of how He spoke and taught and shared with the people He loved. Does my speech ring with grace? It is easy to tell when it doesn't.

"You must get enthusiasm for life, or life is not going to have a lot of enthusiasm for you."

- J. Harold Smith

The cowbell quotient

On our acreage, we have a flock of sheep. We've put a few small, fine, Swiss bells around the necks of a couple of the lead ewes. The bells help scare off any dogs that might come by, and we're alerted to danger when we hear them ringing wildly.

We also placed a plain, old cowbell on one of them. While all the finely tuned Swiss bells make a nice pleasant sound, the cowbell just clanks. I don't have the best ear for music, but even I can hear the difference and it irritates me. I have left that cowbell on that ewe as a daily reminder to monitor how I speak.

Does my family enjoy talking to me? Does my speech warm them up? Do people gladly hear what I have to say? Or does my voice just clank?

When I was younger in my faith, Mom once asked me why I had such an annoyed attitude about life. She wondered why I sounded so angry all of the time. She said that I sounded like I had a chip on my shoulder, even when I was talking about my faith.

Her comment was humbling and I felt a little ashamed.

Sometimes as dads, we can think that our primary mission in

life is to point out what's wrong with this world. But that's the Holy Spirit's job. As fathers, at times we are called on to reconcile our families with one another. But reconciliation is always "good news."

I am thankful that Mom doesn't tell me that I sound angry any more. We never know what burdens people might already be carrying, so we should be careful when we open our mouths.

Our motto should be: Speak softly and forget the big stick.

Do our friends and associates demonstrate that they enjoy hearing us? Do our family members enjoy our conversation? Or are we always correcting people and sounding like that clanking cowbell?

You can read someone's interest and spirit in his eyes. It is a dead give-away, if we'll only look for it.

As teachers, whether at home or in front of an audience outside of our homes, I am concerned about this quality of speech – whether my audience is an audience of one or one hundred and one.

Would people make sacrifices to hear what we have to say? Do our family members go out of their way to hear from us? They will if our message "rings" with grace.

I heard a good joke the other day and at the risk of boring you, here it is. (Your specific need at this moment may be to just grin a little.)

It's Sunday morning and the son tells his mother over breakfast that he just doesn't want to go to church. When she asks for an explanation, he answers, "Mom, I have two reasons. I don't like them and they don't like me." To which his mother responds, "Well, son, I have two reasons why you ought to go. First, you're 45 years old – and second, you're the pastor."

Did that make you smile? I hope so. It pokes a little fun at our insecurities and yet it does so with grace. It "radiates a little grace," so to speak. Do we laugh with our spouse and with the kids? And radiate a little grace?

Matthew Henry writes, "Even when our message is not directly *about* the grace of God, our speech should always be filled *with* the grace of God." (Mr. Henry wrote commentaries on the Bible and did so in such a gracious way that he is read today, even though he died a long time ago.)

Good stories can be very encouraging, especially when they first lift our spirits. I have laughed at the same old jokes for years – sometimes because I simply enjoy the brother who is sharing it and how he tells it. Laugh with your kids. Tell those crazy family stories over and over again.

"Let no unwholesome word proceed from your mouth, but only such a word as is good for edification according to the need of the moment, that it may give grace to those who hear."

- Ephesians 4:29

The word "unwholesome" brings to mind something that is polluted or unsafe to eat. This Scripture teaches that these kinds of words are not safe even to speak. Don't let them come out of your mouth. Rather seek to make the people around you smile.

"Now no one after lighting a lamp covers it over with a container, or puts it under a bed; but he puts it on a lamp stand, in order that those who come in may see the light."

- Luke 8:16

Your kids are watching

We need to be smiling. But what's there to smile about? Do we have anything inside that wants to shine through? I ask myself often, during busy times, whether I am enjoying myself, truly enjoying these days that God has given me. Is there something good going on in my heart? Does it want to get out?

Arthur Rubinstein once said, "You cannot play the piano well, unless you are singing in your heart." Am I experiencing a joyful life – a singing, joyful heart – as a believing Christian dad?

If I am singing deep down in the middle of my soul, then I will be able to "play it well." I will live and display the Christian life more effectively before the people in my life.

I cannot remember who made the following statement – "God's greatest Christians have always been the merriest-hearted" – but I believe it! You can't communicate what you don't have inside. So, are we happy?

Our message as fathers to our families must be faith-filled, joyful, and chock full of light.

Sometimes I think we imagine that our message as fathers should be one of doom and sacrifice. And we then wonder why so few of our children respond to our message – or even want to be with us.

Our message must be infectiously positive and Christ-centered, based around the One who has great and lasting answers for this broken world.

And first and always, we must daily demonstrate that we know the One who "has the whole world in His hands."

Remember we can't live this life and please God unless we are singing in our hearts.

Goodness, goodness, that is so true.

I must share another great quote, this one by Charles H. Spurgeon. He focuses in on some of these same thoughts when he said, "I would not give much for your Christianity unless it can be seen. Lamps do not talk, but they do shine." I wholeheartedly agree!

As we put even more emphasis upon our "shining," I am sure that our Lord will continue to increase our effect and testimony before our kids. It is so easy to be concerned with having the answers and knowing what to say, when more proper concern needs to be placed on the quality of life we are showing our families.

Kids are attracted to light and real life, shown by parents who are faith-filled.

Earlier this year I was studying out the word "witness" in the Bible. One definition that caught my attention was "to win a hearing." In other words, to witness means to live our lives in such a way that people, including our kids, will listen to our message. All we need to do is shine, and shine brightly enough that we will win a hearing from them.

A dad's all-important role

The following illustration about a father's role in transmitting standards to his children comes from a message delivered by fellow dad Norm Wakefied at a conference in Des Moines, Iowa, awhile back.

My wife had just been talking on the phone with another mother, a lady we have been counseling. She and her husband have been going through a devastating time. Their oldest child is in the midst of a terrible divorce; she is now separated from her husband and living at home with them. Her marriage had hardly lasted a year. You could see it coming.

The mother said that she could see it coming by the time her daughter was three.

The mother told her daughter, "I have watched you all

these years and you have not respected and submitted to your dad."

The daughter responded, "Mom, you were always the one giving me the law and giving out the standards... Dad never seemed to have those standards."

The dad finally spoke up and said to his daughter, "I did have those same standards. It was just that your mom... spoke them."

Dad had the standards, but didn't communicate them. I wonder why?

Was it because the mom was a better communicator? Did he think, "I'll just sit back and let my wife speak for us?"

How do the children take it when Mom does most of the communicating?

Listen, children know inherently inside – God has written it in their hearts – that the Word of God is to come to their family through their father.

The standards are to come through Dad and be communicated by Dad. When a father does this, his children will receive it and respect him as a man. And they will respect other future men in their lives.

But if the standards and the Word of God only come through their mother, the children will eventually disrespect both their mother and their father.

The reason for this is that they will see their mother not submitting to their father. She will be the one leading in the home. And the next thing you will see is the daughter or the son rejecting authority because the father has not patterned things correctly. He is not leading.

Why is the father not leading? The reason this father was not leading is because his leadership came under attack. He compared himself to his wife and he thought he had to be a gifted speaker to communicate God's Word. Even though he knew God's Word, he did not communicate it.

There was also a lot the father didn't know – and a lot he didn't bother to find out. He just figured that if he raised his children in the church and saw that they were schooled, they would all turn out okay.

That is a lie – not the truth. The key is the father being the leader.

Many of us dads want to be leaders for God, but few of us have really counted the cost. It will take all we have and require a certain kind of action that will push us well beyond our comfort zone.

The cost of leadership

Years ago, I remember seeing a good movie about a young man and his coming of age. The central theme of the film was the boy's quest for a "master" willing to train him in the skills he lacked. Let me tell you a portion of the story.

The boy, who'd shown much promise and natural ability, was still brash and overconfident. Early in the movie, this would-be disciple asks a wise and experienced master to teach him all that he has learned in life, to become his master. But the old man, judging that the boy is still too rough around the edges, refuses. The boy then earnestly begins pleading with the master to train him.

In one especially pivotal scene, the master seems to be vacillating. Should he tutor the boy or not? As the youth continues his pleading, the old man gets increasingly irritated and begins to turn away.

"Please train me," the boy implores, in a final attempt to

win the master's favor. "I am not afraid."
The old man turns, and suddenly stares straight into the boy's heart.
"You will be," he declares. "You will be."
Then he turns away again, leaving the lad confused and bewildered.
Does this mean that the master will train him? Should he be happy or scared? The words sounded so ominous.
As the story unfolds, we see the master taking the boy on as an apprentice and beginning his training. And yes, the boy is put through frightening experiences that prove a severe challenge to his determination and persistence. As his training progresses, he realizes that the cost of becoming a leader is much greater than he thought.

Many young Christian men desire to be leaders. Leaders at work, at home, and in the church. They want to be trained, to grow, to be used in the Lord's work. Actually, this should be *every* man's desire, shouldn't it?

We all want to be more effective in our leadership with our loved ones, within our marriages and towards our offspring. But not all of us have seriously stopped to sit down and count the cost of attaining this kind of leadership. We're often like the young man in the movie. We desire to be trained, but we don't realize just what that training will require of us.

I'd like to elaborate on this cost, but first I'd like to briefly examine what's required of leaders in this world and contrast those requirements with leadership in the church and in our homes.

If you desire to be a leader in business, you must possess and display a certain amount of business acumen. However, success at the office doesn't require success on the home front. You can do well at work and still leave your family in shambles.

If you desire to be a leader in sports, you must possess a strong body and a strong will. You'll need to train and condition yourself to perform well. Yet no one really cares about your moral behavior off the field. Whether or not you have a problem with alcohol or drugs or are abusive in speech or selfish at home, won't be evaluated when you're catching the winning touchdown pass.

If you desire to be a leader in science or research, you must know your field and invest long hours in the lab. Yet no one cares whether you can share your findings in an interesting, lively and informative manner. *The clumsy acceptance speeches of the last 20 Nobel Prize winners bear this out all too clearly.*

No matter what profession or arena of leadership we focus on in this world, the field will not require as much of a man, in as many different ways, as the Lord requires of His men for leadership in the church and in the home.

God's men must be strong physically, mentally and morally. *In fact, God's leaders must do and be more than all the leaders in every other sphere of influence combined!*

In the world's system, an athlete must be able to take direction and coaching and do what he is told. God's "athlete" must be able to accept coaching, also. But, in addition, he must also be a self-starter. He must train and practice when there's no coach to spark him to do it. God's man is the one who initiates to study God's Word to "show himself approved" when no one is watching. He knows how to begin something and he knows how to persevere when he is all alone.

Many corporations work on the team concept, where everyone in an entire department or division works on a project together, and in turn, everyone involved receives either the benefits or the blame for the outcome. God's leaders must also be able to work together as a team and display a genuine submission towards one another. However, God's men must also often work alone.

Do you desire to be a better leader in your home? Then know this: You will experience times of severe testing and trial. If you think that you are not afraid, rest assured: "You will be."

My desire is not to drive men away from leadership by saying this. I definitely desire for more and more men to be leaders in their homes. I wish that hundreds of men would "set their faces like flint" to become better leaders this very year. Stronger leaders before their wives.

At the same time, I recognize that a healthy response to realizing the demands of our job is to exclaim like Paul, "Who is adequate for these things?" (2 Corinthians 2:16). It's comforting to see how Paul answers his own question, later in the next chapter. He writes, "Our adequacy is from God... who made us adequate."

Adequate means "sufficient for a particular job." God is the one who makes us into men who are sufficient for the task. It's His business to raise up His leaders. He looks for men with eager, willing spirits who are able to listen. Men who will ask the Master – and keep asking the Master – to train them.

I pray that we will all prove to be such men.

(Oh and by the way, if it will help you guess the movie title, the young boy's name was Luke.)

Chapter 20 - Discussion Questions

1. How *"old"* is your faith? Is it fresh and alive? How will you keep it polished and attractive, like a well-used pearl?

2. How does your speech sound? Optimistic and full of grace? Or critical and annoying like that *"clanking cowbell"*? How is your "merry heart" and the smile on your face?

3. Ask your spouse and your kids these questions about your life.

4. For you dads, are you leading or are you letting your wife do the majority of the speaking for you?

5. *"God's men must be strong physically, mentally and morally. In fact, God's leaders must do and be more than all the leaders in every other sphere of influence combined!"* Does this statement intimidate you or inspire you...or both? Why? Ask God for a promise from His Word to cling to for inspiration and strength (e.g., 2 Corinthians 2:14, 3:4-5, Joshua 1:5-9).

21
Honoring our Parents

We're all familiar with the commandment that says to "honor your father and your mother." But I am not going to talk about us getting this kind of honor from our kids.

Instead I am going to talk about how well we are "patterning" this principle to our kids in honoring our own folks. Our example in honoring our parents will speak volumes to our own children and help them to do likewise.

So let me start with a story...

It was a warm, lazy, summer afternoon and I was about 14 years old. My brothers and I had been racing each other on foot along a dirt path behind our house in the country.

The sun was going down and supper was nearly ready when Dad turned into our lane in his pickup. He pulled up to where we were, got out and immediately challenged us to a foot race. There were five of us Whitney boys at the time and, starting with the youngest, Dad ran the same sprint with each of us one-on- one. He ran slow enough to make a good race out of it for the younger ones, so as not to discourage any of them. But by the time he started running against us older guys, it was all serious. Still, he beat all four of my brothers, each time, by just about one step.

It was sort of like a nightly ritual. Dad would often come home from work and get involved in whatever we were doing – shooting baskets, doing chores, or running foot races like this night. And always Dad would make it into a lot of fun as we all tried to impress him by showing how fast we were, how far we could jump, or what we had been making or carving or hammering on or digging. Always it was fun and always it was Dad who helped us do the thing a little bit better. He was good at it, kind of like a coach.

So now, right before Mom called us in to eat, Dad and I lined up to run while my brothers all called out together: "Ready... set... go!"

I will never forget that race, because halfway through it I knew that I could beat him. It was actually a little scary. I had never beaten my father at anything and I kind of slowed down at the end, a little sheepishly.

But Dad wouldn't hear of it. He told me to run all out and that we would race again right then and there. We did and I beat him and my world changed forever.

Dad just congratulated me and told me that he was happy that I had finally caught up with him. He didn't say anything more about it again as we went in to eat, but now that my children are older, I realize that he probably thought about it a whole lot more than he let on.

It was a mark of his maturity that all he gave was praise and reassurance.

He probably knew that beating him in that race was harder

on me than anyone else. It was hard because, for the first time in my life, I recognized that my father was mortal, a human being.

Simply human

At some point in our growing up, our dads change in our minds from a sort of god-like being over to the merely heroic, and I think I am safe in saying that for all of us, it is a difficult time. It is also an important time.

The Bible tells us to honor our parents and to respect and love them. It seems so obvious and natural to respect and appreciate a "super dad," but what do we do when we eventually see that even our parents have flaws – that they, too, are simply human?

It is at this very point that God instructs children to "honor your father and your mother, for this is right."

Our parents loved us in spite of our all-too-obvious weaknesses. That is maturity. As we grow in maturity and Christ-likeness ourselves, we too must love our parents in spite of their own shortcomings. Regardless of their weaknesses, we are to love them with no limit. The Bible then promises that "it will go well with us" when we do this very thing. Did you also know that this is the only verse given in the New Testament specifically for children to obey?

What does it mean to honor? The word "honor" literally means to highly prize or value someone – to hold him or her up as extremely valuable or rare. God commands us to do this no matter what our parents are like.

"It's not easy to face the mortality of our dads, of those we have elevated in our hearts and minds over the course of our lives. It is not easy to learn that most difficult of lessons

*that teaches that parents aren't perfect. They are just perfect
to you.* "

- Tim Cavanaugh, a friend and fellow dad

I'm sure that I'm not alone when I confess that I have heard
my very own sons and daughters complain about their parents.
Many times that child is absolutely convinced that he or she has a
legitimate reason not to honor Mom and Dad. Baloney! There is
absolutely no reason for us not to love and honor our parents, and
there are many reasons why we must. The main reason is that
God commands us to. If we don't honor them, we don't honor or
fear God.

Remember the positive
Whoever has difficulty honoring his parents should meditate
on Philippians 4:8: "Whatever is true, whatever is honorable,
whatever is right, whatever is pure, whatever is lovely, whatever
is of good repute, if there is any excellence and if anything worthy
of praise, let your mind dwell on these things." Perhaps it would
help us to list everything our parents have done that is good,
honorable, right, or worthy of praise.

At a bare minimum, our moms probably changed at least 2,000
of our diapers and cooked 10,000 of our meals. They would
often times be up all night when we cried, and worried sick when
we were ill. Most of our dads worked at least 32,000 hours to
support us while we were growing up. Even the worst parents
have some good qualities, and according to Philippians 4:8, we
should meditate and reflect on only what is good.

Once I heard a young woman say, "But you don't know my
Dad. He is so selfish. He never took any interest in us at all." I
could only point her toward our Savior's example when He said,

"Father, forgive them. They don't really know what they are doing."
If you know Christ as your personal Savior and Lord, you of all
people ought to know about forgiveness and what unconditional
love is. How Christ treats us is how we can and should treat our
parents.

However, even though I knew the truth of these commands
from the Bible, I did not always obey them.

I remember one particular day at work that I got pretty angry
at Dad and yelled at him. Throughout the rest of the day I was
miserable, but I tried to shrug it off. Fat chance. The Lord kept
convicting me that I needed to apologize and tell Dad that I was
sorry for blowing up. God kept reminding me of that simple verse
on honor. I kept justifying my actions by reminding the Lord that
Dad also got mad. It wasn't just my fault. However, after a lot of
internal debate, I gave in, obeyed and apologized to him.

Tell them

"Honor your father and mother, for this is right." The spirit of
obeying this verse involves more than merely doing what is right.
It involves going out of our way to acknowledge our parents with
praise. It involves being generous in our thankfulness toward them.
We need to be creative in honoring our folks.

Once, my grandparents were visiting on Mother's Day and
we were all together for a family reunion of sorts. Everyone was
sitting around the dining room table talking and laughing and
carrying on when my Grandpa stopped everything by quietly taking
both of my Mom's hands in his and looking at them. When we
saw what he did, we all got really quiet. Mom started getting a
little self-conscious and she finally asked Grandpa what was going
on.

Grandpa said that he wished he could understand it.

"Understand what, Bubba?" she asked.

He finally said, "How can such tiny, delicate hands do such an incredible amount of work?" As Mom blushed, he went on to praise her in front of all five of us sons, for all her work and patience in raising us rascals.

I wished that I had been the one to say those words. We need to be generous and vocal in our praise toward our parents.

First priority

When I was 21, I accepted Christ as my personal Savior. I can honestly testify that I love my parents more today that I ever have. However, with this love for my folks has also come a great love for the Lord and awareness of my responsibilities to Him. My relationship with my parents has grown as I have wrestled with my first priority: my love for Christ.

Let me share an example.

Two years after I became a Christian, I began to grapple with a major change in my life's direction. I had always planned to work right alongside Dad for the rest of my life, raising cattle and a family. But the more I read my New Testament, the more I saw that God had a task for me that only a believer could attempt. That was and is to reach the world with the message of eternal life through Jesus Christ. I recognized that I needed to join with other Christians who were seeking to do this and that involved moving away from my hometown and family.

That was hard on my parents, but it was even harder for me. All this time that I was growing more and more convinced that the Lord wanted me to "walk worthy of His name," I was also growing closer to my Dad. We aren't that outwardly demonstrative, but both of us had learned how to hug each other and had even cried together over a few decisions.

And now the hardest decision was to move away.

My Dad sat me down in his warehouse in town one day and

began to tell me very directly that I should be very careful in making this decision to follow the Lord, now that I had a wife and greater responsibilities. I appreciated his concern and felt that I had never loved him more than at that moment. But I also knew that I loved the Lord even more. I told Dad that I felt God wanted me to step out in faith in order to teach us both that one of His greatest characteristics is that He is a provider.

Two Loves

Dad then went on to mention how hard it would be for Mom if my wife Neva and I moved at this time. Only five months earlier one of my brothers had been killed in a car wreck. God had used his death to drive home to me the reality of eternity and I had not missed His point. I mentioned this to Dad and shared how Jesus said, "Night is coming when no man can work" (John 9:4).

The problem seemed to be that God had given me two opposing loves. I loved my parents more than ever, yet I loved the Lord even more and this love seemed to be pulling me in two different directions. Yet in Proverbs it says, "A righteous son makes his father glad."

Sometimes in the short run, obedience to God may seem to be hurting the very ones we love so much. But in the long run, it always strengthens our relationships with them.

However we feel, we must first be righteous and obedient to our Savior. I thought of our Lord's example when His mother and brothers came for Him because they thought He had lost His senses. Even when everyone in His family thought He was wrong, He stuck by His convictions and served His heavenly Father first (Mark 3:21, 31-35).

As a boy of 12, Jesus was under His parents' authority and He obeyed them. Later, as a grown man, He had to make choices that seemed to go against His mother's wishes. However, as

Jesus honored His heavenly Father, God gave Him back his earthly mother and brothers; they were all in the upper room at Pentecost as part of the beginning of the New Testament church.

Jesus always honored and loved His mother. Even from the cross, he took steps to ensure that she would be lovingly taken care of, after He died. Yet not for one instant did He veer from His duty to carry out God's sacrifice. Nor should we.

I believe that as a result of my obedience to the Lord, God has graciously given me a better relationship with my folks than I have ever had – or ever would have had.

Example wins

Our Lord asks us to live out a strong, clear, gentle witness to our parents. At times this involves some hard decisions, a whole lot of service and a genuine lifestyle to back it up. Throw in a little sharing of the gospel and you have a winning combination.

Our parents know us better than anyone. We need to demonstrate the genuine fruit of a changed life as our opening message to our folks. We sometimes believe that we can bluff a stranger with the gospel message apart from a changed life. But don't even think that you can do this with your parents.

Have you ever seriously prayed and thought about not only being a positive influence to your folks for Christ but also seeing them joining you in the work of sharing the gospel? I have.

I would encourage you to spend some time thinking about this. In the past, Mom and Dad have both kind of chuckled when I brought it up. I have told them how I planned to have them join me and they both tried to put me off by saying how there could not possibly be any room for a couple of older people in what I was doing.

Then I showed them many exciting examples in the Bible where God enlisted men into His service, even after they had grown older. They no longer laugh at my idea any more.

I also wanted them to know that I would certainly take care of them when they grew old. I Timothy 5:6 speaks of meeting the needs of our own. We should let our folks know that there will always be room in our homes for them when they are no longer able to take care of themselves.

I trust that God will give all of us greater grace in this exciting work of learning how to love and honor our folks. And that our folks would see that we love and honor them because God has called us to.

Because we are God's best evidence and witness to our family.

Chapter 21 - Discussion Questions

1. How honoring are you to your own parents (and to your spouse's)? Have you recently expressed to them your love and appreciation, your commitment to care for them, etc.?

2. Have your children seen you demonstrate honor to your parents, or have they seen dishonor such as complaining about your parents or spouse's parents?

3. How can a greater love for Christ increase your love for your parents?

22
"Positioning" our Teens

"And these words, which I am commanding you today, shall be on your heart; and you shall teach them diligently to your sons and shall talk of them when you sit in your house and when you walk by the way and when you lie down and when you rise up."

- Deuteronomy 6:6-7

At times, a father will say to me, "Just tell it to me straight, Rick. Keep it simple. What exactly do you insist on when it comes to your own teens? What are some practical habits that you always go back to when you're training your sons and daughters?"

Well, it's pretty straightforward really – I insist that they be "positioned" correctly in life and that they pursue a few practical habits daily to keep them positioned that way. When I talk about them being positioned correctly, I mean that they are:

- First, "positioned" before God
- Second, "positioned" between their God and their friends
- Third, "positioned" alongside other believers as their servant.

This is basically what I insist on when it comes to my teens' growth and progress in the faith. This "positioning" is essential to ensure that a teen keeps his head on straight and stays focused on God throughout his high school years.

Now don't get me wrong. We don't always hit a home run in daily habits in the Whitney household. But this positioning is what we're striving for. If we can get these three mindsets instilled into our children, we can be pretty confident that they will turn out well as teens. I have yet to see a family build these things into their children and ultimately fail with their teens. If you can get them – and keep them – in the right position, you can't go wrong.

So let's take a closer look at some practical habits that reinforce this positioning.

Habit #1: Journaling

I insist that my children journal every day. Not just read their Bible, but also write something down at the end of their reading time. I insist that they respond to God by writing down what they think God is trying to say to them. This "positions" them before their God.

Reading is not enough; they need to be writing – and writing every day. Writing helps ensure that they are not just staring at a page, but actually hearing something from their Savior. (At least it gets them a lot closer to hearing.) Teach them to write! English teachers insist on it and get it almost every week, and we've got a lot more invested in our kids than they do.

I know journaling isn't necessarily easy. It can be hard work, especially for boys. Well, dads, it is our job to make our kids do the things their flesh doesn't want to do. Our flesh doesn't always like certain duties either, but we learn to do them anyway. Doing things you don't like to do is part of growing up. It just goes with the turf.

So stick with it, dads. Keep encouraging your kids in this, even when you don't always bat a thousand. It's critically important to your teenager's future and puts him or her in the same right "position" before God as the Old Testament writer who said, "Here am I, Lord!"

Habit #2: Praying for lost friends

I insist that my children pray every day for their lost friends. They each carry a 3x5 card in their Bible with the names of three lost friends that God has put on their heart. I insist that they pray for these friends daily and seek God that they might be saved. This "positions" them between their God and their friends.

This kind of intercessory prayer trains their hearts. It teaches them to look on their classmates as lost sheep to be won, rather than as peers to impress. It helps them to see themselves as "princes among thieves." This is just the mindset God wants them to have as they go about making those countless daily choices in life. They need to realize that they weren't created just to play video games and hang out at the mall, but to "stand in the gap" between their friends and their God.

Sometimes our kids would rather just "fit in" and not be on a mission. (Let's face it, we adults can relate. Sometimes we'd rather just kick back and relax, too.) But it's our job as dads to encourage them – by our words and our example – to be aware that they are on this earth to make an eternal difference in people's lives, to be involved in literally "snatching them out of the fire" as the New Testament puts it. This is vitally important, men. This is where the rubber meets the road, especially with our teens.

Habit #3: Showing up to serve

I insist that my children serve other believers every week. I require that they go to church and youth group – whether they feel like it or not. And I insist that they attend for what they can put into it, not just for what they feel they can get out of it. This "positions" them alongside their fellow Christians as a servant.

Through the years, all of the family conversations we've had before and after church and before and after teen group have centered around one thing: modeling a mindset of serving others. Each time we ask ourselves, "How did we help? How could we make it better?" In this way, we demonstrate to our teens how they need to look on fellow Christians as their betters and to view Christian gatherings as times to serve, not just as times to pal around with their friends.

Sometimes our teens think that church is boring; sometimes they would rather not go to youth group. Would we let them stay home from school just because they were "bored" with history or they "didn't feel like" going to algebra class? No way. End of discussion. It's not even an option! In the same way, we can't let our teens' attitudes or responses dictate our behavior as parents.

When our teens balk or whine about attending youth group or church, this is our time to step in and train them, dads. This is our golden opportunity to teach them not to be proud, but to be a servant to God's people. Like the Bible says, "So you too, when you do all the things which are commanded you, should say, 'We are unworthy slaves; we have done only that which we ought to have done.'" This habit is crucial to our teens' spiritual growth.

For example, when we see that they attend church – whether they want to be there or not – we are really putting them in front of God's Spirit. Who knows what God might do?! Our Lord is often a "Holy Spirit freight train" and can break through to the dullest or most closed of hearts.

Occasionally a dad will say to me, "My boy doesn't like to write. My boy likes to hang with his 'buds.' My boy is tired and bored with church." (In other words, his boy doesn't want to be in position.) My gut reaction is, "Remember, dad, it is not your role to adapt to the wishes of your children, but to conform them to the wishes of your God."

Requiring these three simple habits of my children has side benefits, too. As my kids have faithfully modeled these godly mindsets – whether they wanted to or not – it has built discipline and obedience into their lives as well.

So for our teens, getting them positioned is everything. Because the stakes are high. In fact, as the following story – taken from Dennis Rainey's book, Parenting Today's Adolescent – illustrates, the stakes are even higher than we might realize:

Stepping through the traps

The scene caused a chill to trickle down my back. On an outdoor stage in Denver, Colorado, with fifty thousand Promise Keepers watching intensely, a fifteen-year-old boy – blindfolded and barefoot – began stepping cautiously toward a dangerous obstacle course filled with a dozen steel animal traps. Directly in front of the boy lay the grim, gray jaws of a huge bear trap that was so powerful that it could crush his leg and so large that setting it had required three men. Several feet to the left of the bear trap lay a smaller device, a beaver trap – quick and potent. Next to me, twenty-five feet away from the blindfolded young man, stood the boy's father.

This unusual demonstration was my closing illustration in a message entitled "Turning Your Heart toward Your Children." I wanted to make a visual point that children need their dads to guide them through the challenging terrain of adolescence and life. On each of the traps I had fastened labels representing the "traps" of adolescence, words like peer pressure, alcohol, drugs, sexual immorality, rebellion, and pornography.

The boy took two tentative steps and was about to take a third – directly toward the bear trap – when his father Tom screamed into the microphone, "Trent, stop! Don't take another step. I'll be right there!" His order echoed through cavernous Mile High Stadium. The air seemed to suck out of the stadium as an eerie silence replaced the normal fidgeting and low-grade hum of the throng. No one moved. Except Tom.

Trent sure didn't move. He waited obediently as his father circled the trap field and stepped in between his son and the bear trap. Tom whispered instructions to Trent.

Then he turned his back to the boy. The young man eagerly placed his hands on his father's shoulders.

Slowly, taking small and deliberate steps, Tom maneuvered through the trap field, his son nearly glued to his back. Trent's hands gripped Tom's shoulders, his shuffling feet often clipping his dad's heels. Tom stayed as far from the traps as possible, not taking the slightest risk that Trent might bump a trap with his bare toes.

One man's tentative clapping broke the silence in the stadium. Soon others joined in. A chorus of voices yelled encouragement to the father and son. Only a few yards, a few traps remained. When the two reached me and the blindfold was pulled off, Tom and Trent hugged each other. Applause and cheering started at one end of the field and swelled to a thunderous standing ovation, rolling like a tidal wave across the stadium.

Above the roar I shouted over the sound system, "Men, that's what God has called us to as fathers – to guide our

children through adolescence, the most dangerous period of
our children's lives!"

An amazing illustration, yet so fitting. What is at stake with
our sons and daughters is nothing less than their very lives! But I'd
like to contend that there are even more lives at stake than just
our children's lives.

> *Jesus repeated the question:*
> *"Simon son of John, do you love Me?"*
> *"Yes, Lord," Peter said, "You know I love You."*
> *"Then take care of My sheep," Jesus said.*

- John 21:16 NLT

Jesus gave Peter very clear direction. Our Lord said (and I
am paraphrasing), "I want you to get engaged here, Peter. I want
you to get involved with other people. Build the Kingdom, Peter.
Build the church. Take care of My sheep!"

Then the Lord challenged him again: "Do you love Me? I
don't want to just hear about what you feel, Peter. I want to know
what you're willing to do for My lambs. Are you willing to get
involved here? Because that is what I want from you."

There are two immediate, possible applications in these verses
for all of us as fathers.

The first is that we need to love those sheep, those kids that
live in our own home. We surely need to take care of them first
and feed them first.

But I want to focus in on a second, more primary application
– and then zero in on something. The following application is
probably more important to me than anything else when I think
about raising my sons and daughters.

If I am going to succeed as a father, I need to help my teens to personally own this Scripture, and to show it by getting involved in the lives of others.

It must get to the place where I have truly given them the heart and the desire to love others as Jesus directs Peter to love. If our teens would take the place of Peter, then they must not only answer, "Yes, Lord, you know that I love you," but they must also take His instructions to heart and feed His sheep.

Our Lord answers Peter's declaration of love with this simple thought: If you really do love Me, then you'll get involved in taking care of others.

We must succeed in giving this same heart and life perspective to our kids.

I insist on obedience from my kids at all times, and when they are teens, at times it can get kind of messy, even ugly. As a family we also have a ton of fun together. But I am looking for something that goes beyond obedience and beyond fun, something that gets outside of the Whitney household.

God forbid that in this association of churches we would try to save our kids at the expense of the world around us. If we dare believe that we can save our kids – without a concern for our society, our world and our Lord's gospel – then we will not only continue to see our society crumble, but *we will also lose our kids.*

We must give our kids this gospel vision of being involved in, speaking to and sharing with all of God's people. And helping those sheep who are so truly lost.

We must help our children to correctly answer His question: "Do you love Me?"

If their answer doesn't involve a heartfelt commitment to the Great Commission, to His mission and purpose, and to His outward focus, then it is inherently selfish. We must help our teens get beyond this basically selfish, typically American orientation to their faith that is so common throughout Christian society. They must develop and maintain an outward focus.

Mission or omission?

There is this great and glaring omission in all of the parenting books I have read. Not a word is written about being in this world to draw people to Christ in obedience to our Lord's Great Commission.

What I have found on the cover of almost every Christian-oriented book on parenting is a title that goes something like this: SAVE YOUR KIDS! READ THIS BOOK!

Often the hidden, unspoken subtitle is: Forget about the world.

The greatest commandment says to "love the Lord your God" and to "love your neighbor as yourself." And you only have two kinds of neighbors – saved and lost.

Jesus Himself said that all of the Law, all of the Bible studies, all of the church-going, all of the youth group meetings and all of the personal character development that we might engage in – all of it – hinges on obeying this one supreme commandment.

Jesus' summation of the Law involves our vertical relationship with God and also our horizontal relationship with people. We have to truly be involved in people's lives to be obedient to this greatest of all commandments.

Can we personally answer our Lord's question – "Do you love Me?" – with the correct response, that of reaching out to others both inside and outside the church?

If we, as an association of churches, had not sought to obey the second part of His commandment – the part about loving our neighbors, about reaching out with the gospel and trying to help our brother in Christ – then I believe that we would have become the most miserable bunch of weak-willed believers around. We would probably still exist as a group of churches, but most likely we would have become proud.

But thank the Lord that He was gracious and gave us protection through obeying this teaching! We had God-given, God-revealed answers and they guarded us. Without those answers, we easily could have become stagnant. We must give this same spiritual protection, this same outward orientation to our teens if we really hope to "save" them in the end.

God forbid that we raise our kids well – and accept the glory for it for ourselves, our families and our churches – at the expense of those around us who are perishing.

We must give our teens a purpose that is directed outward toward the lost. If we don't, our Christianity will be hollow – and it will look, feel and sound hollow, especially to our own sons and daughters.

If we don't engage our teens to live for a cause that involves the gospel and the lost and all the mess that goes with it – if we don't enlist them with us in this holy struggle – then they will get to a certain point in life and say, "Why am I doing all of this? Mom and Dad, you continually say that you love me and that we all love each other, but why are we here? What is the point of all of this Christian activity?"

The only legitimate way I can answer these questions as a father is to verbally communicate and to physically demonstrate that everything we do as a family is for the sake of the lost.

We need to say – with our words and with our lives – "Your testimony, son, is for the lost. Your opportunities in life, daughter, are for the lost. That is why God put you here. That is why you walk the halls of your high school. For the lost!"

We need to say – with our words and with our lives – "You can either be salt and light in that high school or you can sleepwalk through it and hide out. You can be one kind of Christian on Sunday morning and another kind the rest of the week – or you can be consistent. But you will have to decide, son – you will have to choose, daughter – one path or the other."

A question of loyalty

John Meyer recently reminded us at a teen conference that the crux of our Christianity is not so much a question of our character, as it is a question of our loyalty. To whom are we going to be loyal? If we choose to be loyal to our Savior and His mission and His claim on our lives, proven character will be the inevitable result. Character is the natural byproduct of a fundamentally God-centered orientation, of a basic recognition of who our Captain is and what His wants for our lives.

We must be engaged in this mission, parent. And our children must join us in this same mission, the mission that God gave us to be "salt and light." Tell your sons and daughters that this is the key. This is critical. When my kids were in high school, this conversation outweighed all others.

Our teens are princes among thieves and they need to act accordingly. They must always be thinking of gracious ways to rescue their lost friends who are perishing. They must be praying for souls and on the hunt for lives. You have to coach your kids on how to do this and on how to share their faith.

To do this, they should start with a prayer list. They need to be in prayer for the salvation of their lost friends. Then they need to plan how they can initiate spiritual conversations and try to win those classmates to Christ. Our sons need to think about just what is winsome and what is not. We need to be deliberately coaching them on these things.

Have I taught my teens the simple skills of winning someone's friendship? Do they know how to effectively give someone a gospel tract and how to set up a follow-up conversation? Do they know when to talk about their faith and when not to initiate? Do they know what spiritual topics to avoid while in a group or on a bus or with the team in the locker room? Do they know how to transition a conversation, how to ask the right questions? Are they sensitive to the opportunities that always come when we've been praying?

Can our teens correctly answer our Lord's question: "Do you love Me?" If they aren't answering that question with a demonstrated commitment to the gospel, if they are not putting feet to their words – while they are still in high school – there will come a day when we will grieve because our kids will simply chuck it all. Without an outward focus, they will eventually come to realize that the real purpose of their family's so-called faith was inherently selfish.

Give this outward mission to your kids while you still have the chance, parents. Get your teenage sons and daughters involved in feeding sheep – sheep both saved and lost. It is the only thing that truly matters.

"My church can die, but not my family. My church can die, but not my family...not my family."

- Mark Darling

Chapter 22 - Discussion Questions

1. There are three simple things we should require our teens to do: Journaling, Praying for lost friends, and Showing up to serve. What steps will you and your spouse take to implement these things?

2. What will help you to *"stay at it"* and not give up or forget about it?

3. "If we dare believe that we can save our kids – without a concern for our society, our world and our Lord's gospel – then we will not only continue to see our society crumble, but *we will also lose our kids."* Is your teen progressing in an *"others-orientation"*? Are you? What changes do you need to make?

4. Has your teen been trained yet in sharing his/her faith?

23
How to raise Confident, Beautiful Daughters

"Daughters, I think, are always easier for fathers. I don't know why."

- William Plummer

The other day I was driving somewhere with my daughter, who's a college senior now. While we were talking in the car, she told me that I ought to write an article on how to raise confident, beautiful daughters. I suggested that she write out exactly what she meant, so she did. Here are her thoughts. (Thanks, princess!)

Dear Dad,
As promised, here are some of my thoughts about different issues that affect women, especially teenage women.
I have noticed that a lot of girls in the dorms have this huge lack of confidence. I think there is way too little written about the

issue of how girls are really doing in the area of confidence, even from the church. My classes try to offer answers, but they fail.

We as Christians should be "all over this" because we have the ultimate answers. But in reality, we shy away from it much like the world does.

I think that you would have a lot of authority on this topic of building confident daughters, since you have almost finished raising five confident, beautiful women! ☺

You do a great job of incorporating stories about girls into your teachings, but that is sort of rare. Remember that over fifty percent of your audience is women! Even though pastors and fathers are not females, they need to be aware of the female half of their audience and communicate with them by using illustrations about women more often.

During the last four years, I have had the privilege of leading over 100 female residents here in the dorms as a Resident Assistant (RA). In that time, I've learned a lot of things about girls in our society today. Here are some of them:

- Did you know that our culture seems to see a strengthening and a "flourishing" in girls as they mature, up until they hit adolescence – and then things just go haywire?

- Did you know that the suicide rates for girls peak at age 13 and 14?

- Did you know that at adolescence, girls begin to adopt certain "masks" and want to imitate other people – both their peers and female celebrities like Britney Spears and Jennifer Lopez?

- Did you know that girls who are 16 right now are the first generation to grow up in a culture that is completely image-based?

- Did you know that 80% of girls feel inadequate – physically, intellectually and in many other areas? (Based on my experience in the dorms, I believe it.)

- Did you know that there's this constant drumbeat in the mass media that says that girls have to be attractive and thin? That message comes out through countless images that attack our girls, constantly demanding that they be thinner, have flawless skin, look sexy all the time, etc.

- Did you know that one out of five college-age women has an eating disorder?

- Did you know that 80% of fourth-grade girls are on diets? That's right – *fourth graders!*

- Did you know that one in four college-age women can expect to be the victim of sexual violence and/or abuse sometime in her life?

The list goes on and on, and it just gets worse and worse! I'm convinced that everything I just mentioned is true, because I have seen almost all of these statistics borne out in real life as I've worked with many, many female college students in the dorms.

Anyway, as I sit in some of my classes, I hear this litany of sad and terrible things going on with all of these women that I am trying to lead in the dorms – horrible statistics, heartbreaking stories – and it just ticks me off!

I see girls from broken homes trying to find their identity in boys, in boyfriends and in what boys think of them. In clothes, clothes and more clothes. Many girls are trying to find a healthy self-image by performing in school, sometimes excessively going after the grades, hoping to feel good about themselves. There is no real inner confidence to be found in these things. Yet girls are trying to find value and a sense of worth in such empty, broken ways.

As I look at how I was raised, I can't help but realize how gracious God was to me. I had parents who instilled in me things that were God-honoring and that reflected what God thought of me. He used you two as His "pipeline." I was truly blessed to be Mom's daughter (and yours ☺).

But what does that mean? Specifically how did you two bless me?

You did a lot for us, but these are some of the major things that I think He taught me through you guys:

- You always made me feel beautiful. My four sisters and I all think we are beautiful, because you kept telling us so. (I remember Mom telling me that I was so tall that I could be a model. That helped me never try to hide my height or to be self-conscious about it.)

- You always made me feel protected. One way you did that was by monitoring what we watched on TV, the images that we put into our heads. (And I remember your response, Dad, to those crazy guy residents one year who were trying to intimidate me!)

- You validated our emotions, but taught us to not be controlled by them. You told us at times to shut off the tears.

- You taught us to work hard – and I mean, *really hard.* Harder than most girls I have contact with have ever dreamed of working!

- You taught us not to be "wimpy" or "girlie," but how to get past our fears instead. And you insisted that we get past them.

- You saw to it that we worked outdoors a lot. There wasn't anything that you asked our brothers to do around the acreage, that you didn't ask us girls to do, too.

- You made sure we learned many important things about running a home, like meal planning and preparation and how to do a "Ton of Housework." You insisted that we girls learn how to do all of these things, instead of you both always serving us and doing those things for us.

- You gave us responsibilities in the church all the time. We did a lot of set-up, taught nursery and Sunday school, ran tape libraries, and led in youth group. You name it, we did it.

- You gave us a lot of responsibility. It didn't matter if we were a son or a daughter, you leaned on us.

- You made sure that we did a lot of physical things that helped build courage in each of us. We showed a lot of great market lambs in 4-H. (I remember when one sister almost broke her finger right before show day at the county fair, yet you helped her to still compete and win.)

- You both constantly praised our gifts and talents.

- You always showed us that you loved us. It seems like a lot of fathers are intimidated when their daughters begin to go through puberty and become young women, but I never felt estranged from you. I was always confident in your love for me and for all of my sisters.

• You protected us from dating in high school. _In my opinion, this is so critically and pivotally important!_ A lot could be said here about dating, but you have already said it – over and over and over and over and over. ☺

Anyway, we don't need any more teachings about how not to "arouse or awaken love" or about "guarding our hearts" or about being the "weaker vessel."

What we really need to teach our young women is how to be warriors who will stand beside their brothers and fight with them! We need women who will "stand in the gap" and lay down their lives for the advancement of the Kingdom of God! I want us to be a movement of strong women who don't care what the world tells us is important – women who will stop worrying about their weight and their hair, and care about the salvation of the lost instead!

You and I know that the battle we are fighting is fierce. I firmly believe that the devil attacks our women twice as hard as our men with all of these lies about supposed "inadequacies."

Anyway, these are some of my random thoughts, things I have been praying about since our conversation in the car. I would appreciate your input. I will keep praying.

Love you, Dad,
Joy

Are we raising confident daughters? Are we raising beautiful daughters, daughters who are beautiful according to God's definition of beauty? (I'm talking here about the true beauty that's primarily a product of character and spirit.)

Once in awhile something happens that surprises and encourages us as parents – somewhat like a "roman candle" going off – because we see, maybe for the first time, these very traits in our own daughters.

And often it happens when we least expect it.

My oldest son had just brought his fiancé home for the first time. We were all sitting around the dinner table, all nine of us and our special guest. It was a big deal for my daughters; they were a little nervous to meet Krista in this special way. After dinner we stayed at the table talking and somehow the conversation got around to old school lessons of the past.

Literature, poetry, topics that are not usually on the docket. Neva wondered if the kids remembered a few special poems, and asked for a few volunteers to recite. One boy worked through the lines to the poem "If" by Rudyard Kipling. The other launched into the classic speech that William Wallace gave to his troops in the movie "Braveheart."

Then out of the blue, Jessica, our second youngest, announced to all nine of us big lugs that she would like to recite the poem "Opportunity" by Edward Roland Sills. Whereupon she pushed her chair back from the table, climbed up on it, and began – with great flair and strong hand gestures – to share these words:

This I beheld, or dreamed it in a dream:
There spread a cloud of dust along a plain;
And underneath the cloud, or in it, raged
A furious battle, and men yelled, and swords
Shocked upon swords and shields. A prince's banner
Wavered, then staggered backward, hemmed by foes.
A craven hung along the battle's edge,
And thought, "Had I a sword of keener steel –

That blue blade that the king's son bears – but this
Blunt thing!" he snapped and flung it from his hand,
And lowering crept away and left the field.
Then came the king's son, wounded sore bestead,
And weaponless, and saw the broken sword,
Hilt-buried in the dry and trodden sand,
And ran and snatched it, and with battle shout
Lifted afresh he hewed his enemy down,
And saved a great cause that heroic day.

I had never heard Jessica ever do anything like this before. She recited the entire poem as though she were rallying her troops. We all kept smiling and sinking lower and lower in our chairs, quailing before her bold spirit.

She was into it big time! All confidence, all pizzazz. I looked from my end of the table down at Neva on the other end. We both had trouble believing she was doing this. Was this our Jessica? She had always been pretty quiet as a rule, and yet this day she simply erupted with this great speech.

Are our daughters confident? Do we see it? Do they ever show us that they are getting over some of the personal mountains, fears, and anxieties that might multiply even in a young heart?

If we don't see courage, if there is no evidence of confidence, we need to help them by giving them opportunities to risk embarrassment and to step outside of their comfort zones.

The following true story – entitled "Something She Had to Do!" – is reprinted from an excellent article by Bill Sanders. It features a courageous young girl who steps out of her comfort zone and deals with the all-too-real issue of peer pressure. It is an inspiring story and one I just had to include in this chapter on raising confident, beautiful daughters.

It started when she was in the seventh grade, with the doctor's report. Everything that her family had feared was true. The diagnosis – leukemia! The next few months were filled with regular visits to the hospital. She was poked and jabbed and tested hundreds and thousands of times. Then came the chemotherapy. Along with it, and a chance to possibly save her life, she lost her hair.

Losing your hair as a seventh grader is a devastating thing. The hair didn't grow back. The family started to worry.

That summer before her eighth grade year, she bought a wig. It felt uncomfortable, it was scratchy, but she wore it. She was very popular and loved by so many students. She was a cheerleader and always had other kids around her, but things seemed to change. She looked strange, and you know how kids are. I guess maybe like the rest of us...

Sometimes we go after laughter and do things even though it causes great pain in someone else. The wig was pulled off from behind about a half dozen times in the first two weeks of the eighth grade. She would stop, bend down, shake from fear and embarrassment, put her wig back on, wipe away the tears and walk to class, always wondering why no one stood up for her.

This went on for two agonizing, hellish weeks. She told her parents she couldn't take it anymore. They said, "You can stay home if you wish." You see, if your daughter is dying in the eighth grade, you don't care if she makes it to the ninth. Having her happy and giving her a chance at peace is all that matters.

Nikki told me that to lose her hair is nothing. She said, "I can handle that." She even said that losing her life is of little concern. "I can handle that, too," she said, "but do you know what it's like to lose your friends? To walk down the hall and have them part like the 'Red Sea' because you're coming? To go into the cafeteria on pizza day, our best meal, and have them leave with half-eaten plates? They say that they're not hungry but you know that they're leaving because you're sitting there? Do you know what it's like to have no one want to sit next to you in math class and the kids in the locker to the left and right of you have pulled out? They're putting their books in with someone else, all because they might have to stand next to the girl wearing the wig, the one with the weird disease. It's not even catching. They can't get it from me. Don't they know that I need my friends most of all?"

"Oh, yes," she said, "losing your life is nothing when you know where you're going to spend eternity. Losing your hair is nothing either, but losing your friends is so devastating."

She had planned to stay home from school, but something happened that weekend. She heard about two boys – one in the sixth grade, one in the seventh – and the stories gave her the courage to go on.

The seventh-grader was from Arkansas and even though it wasn't popular, he took his New Testament Bible in his shirt to school. As the story goes, three boys approached him, grabbed the Bible and said, "You sissy. Religion is for sissies. Prayer is for sissies. Don't ever bring this Bible back to school again." He reportedly handed the Bible back to the biggest one of the three and said, "Here. See if you've got enough courage to carry this around school just one day." They said that he made three friends that day.

The next story that inspired Nikki was about a sixth-grader from Ohio named Jimmy. He was jealous of California because California had a state motto, "Eureka!" Ohio didn't have any. He came up with six life-changing words. He single-handedly got enough signatures. With his petitions full, he took it before the State Legislature. Today, because of a brave sixth-grader, the official state motto for Ohio is "All things are possible with God."

With Nikki's newfound courage and inspiration, she put her wig on that next Monday morning. She got dressed as pretty and fancy as she could. She told her mom and dad, "I'm going back to school today. There's something I've got to do. There's something I've got to find out." They didn't know what she meant and they were worried, fearing the worst, but they drove her to school.

Every day for the last several weeks, Nikki would hug and kiss her mom and dad in the car before she got out. As unpopular as this was and even though many kids sneered and jeered at her, she never let it stop her. Today was different. She hugged and kissed them, but as she got out of the car, she turned quietly and said, "Mom and Dad, guess what I'm going to do today?" Her eyes were filling up with tears, but they were tears of joy and strength. Oh, yes, there was fear of the unknown, but she had a cause.

They said, "What, baby?"

She said, "Today I'm going to find out who my best friend is. Today I'm going to find out who my real friends are."

And with that she grabbed the wig off her head and she set it on the seat beside her. She said, "They take me for how I am, Daddy, or they don't take me at all. I don't have much time left. I've got to find out who they are today." She started to walk, took two steps, then turned and said, "Pray for me."

Her parents responded, "We are, baby." And as she walked toward 600 kids, she could hear her dad say, "That's my girl."

A miracle happened that day. She walked through the playground, into that school, and not one loudmouth or bully, no one, made fun of the little girl with all the courage.

Nikki has taught thousands of people to be yourself, to use your own God-given talent, and to stand up for what is right even in the midst of uncertainty, pain, fear and persecution. This is the only true way to live.

Nikki has since graduated from high school. The marriage that was never supposed to take place happened a few years later, and Nikki is the proud mother of a little girl.

Every time something that seems impossible comes before me, I think of Nikki and I gain strength.

Pretty inspiring story, huh? True courage is a life-changing thing.

Some of our kids just seem to be born with courage and confidence. Others don't. When they don't have it naturally, I am convinced that we parents can build it into their lives. And when they're born with it, we need to recognize that it still needs a lot of shaping and refining. And we can help there, too. Let me illustrate with one last story.

My oldest daughter went off to public school as an eighth-grader. She came home on the bus after the first day of class and some of the first words out of her mouth were, "I'm going to be the valedictorian of my class." After the first day of public school, I guess she wasn't very impressed.

I told her, "That's fine, honey. It's good to have a goal."

She answered, "No, Dad. I'm going to be the valedictorian."

I turned to Neva and said, "She's your daughter."

Anyway, five years later she was class valedictorian and getting ready to graduate. The principal of the high school called her in and said, "Mandy, I know your dad is a preacher and that you are a preacher's daughter, but please do not mention anything religious in your valedictory speech. It might offend those who are not religious. I'm sure you understand."

She didn't understand at all.

She came home very angry and told us, "I'm going to pray through my whole speech, just to show them."

We said, "Settle down, honey. Pray about it." And so she did.

She worked on her speech and we heard a good percentage of it – several times – as she practiced it in the garage. Finally, the big day came.

You have to understand that Amanda is very passionate about her Savior and very indignant when people do not respect her Lord, her faith or her fellow believers. Neva and I weren't exactly sure what was going to happen.

She went up to the podium and began her speech. After working through the usual points on behalf of her fellow students – thanking their teachers, thanking their parents, thanking each other for their friendships – she said, "And in conclusion, I would like to thank someone else..."

I turned to Neva and said, "Here it comes."

Then Mandy showed real nerve and leadership. Here's what she said:

"This week, I was fortunate enough to receive a scholarship from the Denver Broncos. There were over 500 applicants, and they chose twelve of us. The only question the Broncos asked me to respond to on the scholarship application was: 'How would you improve society?'"

"I said that the only way we can improve society is if we acknowledge God."

"Why am I telling you this? If a Denver Bronco football player can thank God for helping him score a touchdown by praying on one knee in the end zone on national TV, I know I

can thank Him for helping get us through high school."

"So lastly, I just want to take a second and publicly thank my personal Savior for all He has done for me."

Then she bowed her head and said, "Thank You, Lord."

Whereupon everyone – all 2,000 people, including the principal – began to applaud. Mandy had scored a touchdown in their hearts by combining God and the Denver Broncos, a sure-fire recipe for pleasing any crowd here in Colorado. Neva and I were, of course, very proud.

Are our daughters confident? Are they truly beautiful in God's sight?

We can instill this kind of spirit in them if we stay engaged as parents and keep building into their hearts and into their minds both a fear of God and courage before man.

Chapter 23 – Discussion Questions

1. "I want us to be a movement of strong women who don't care what the world tells us is important – women who will stop worrying about their weight and their hair, and care about the salvation of the lost instead!"

How does Joy's list of 13 lessons she learned from her parents spark our thinking on how to build confidence in our own daughter's life?

2. Discuss this list with your wife and organize these goals according to the priority needs in the life of your own daughter.

3. Have your daughter read the chapter with you, and then discuss it with her.

24
A few thoughts from
my "*Better Half*"

Author's Note: I asked Neva if she would share from her perspective, on this topic of parenting. Every time I travel folks mention to me how much they enjoy her writing. So I thought I would give Nev some time in this book to *"weigh in"* - from her side. What follows are several of her <u>Daylights</u> entries that deal with parenting.

(<u>Daylights</u> is a daily devotional published by our association of churches.)

These are a few snapshots of our family, and what God has taught my wife in raising our kids. (Neva probably should have written this whole book!)

Mom, what if it doesn't come up?

"Now faith is the assurance of things hoped for, the conviction of things not seen."

- Hebrews 11:1

It had taken a couple hours but we had done it! One spring, on a beautiful afternoon, Grace and I had worked hard and planted our garden.

Now I love most all aspects of gardening. I actually enjoy the weeding, the hoeing, the harvesting, and the eating. The only thing I don't enjoy is planting the seeds. It takes so long and you have to be so careful to get the rows even halfway straight.

We had tried to do it right. We made up a plan ahead of time, thinking about which plants to put next to each other depending upon how tall they would get and how fast they grow. We had our stakes, our string and a yardstick. We were going to have relatively straight rows this year.

As I surveyed the freshly planted garden plot, thankful that the task was completed, Grace said, "Mom, what if it doesn't come up?"

"Not come up! That's impossible. It will come up. We put lots of mulch on the soil. We had it tilled. We'll water it if it doesn't rain. The sun is nice and warm. It will come up," I assured her.

Then I thought of Hebrews 11 and the example of faith involved in planting a garden. I am assured that this garden will come up, yet it takes faith to walk away from it and give it time to grow and to develop. My gardens always come up.

So too in growing my family. Kids do grow up. Children mature and develop and become a part of His kingdom. We just need faith.

Prayer and Character Goals for the Kids

"Not one of the good promises which the Lord had made to the house of Israel failed; all came to pass."

- Joshua 21:45

When I first heard John Hopler speak on "Seven Days of Prayer for our Families," it disturbed me. I knew I didn't always have Christ-like values and character in my life. How could I expect my kids to have this?

And how could I be held accountable for the salvation of all my descendants? That was overwhelming.

And the prayer goal about spouses and mates for my kids. Wow! That really got me. I don't even want to begin thinking about them dating, why should I pray about future mates for them?

Even with all the initial negative reactions on my part, I taped John's little card to my prayer notebook, right next to the list of seven character goals Rick and I have been working and praying to see developed in our children's lives. They are called "Building Blocks" and we want them established in our children lives before they leave our home.

For instance, we are working to see our children love and respect the Bible and know the Bible's stories. Our character goals for the kids include such things as being loyal and eager to serve.

I now pray through these two lists routinely for my family. And as I have been praying for my family, God has given me some insight.

It isn't me who is going to do it all! That thought encouraged me to continue to claim promises for my children and to camp on them. And then I can just leave the outcome to God.

As the years go by, my children will be out on their own. Praying for them has given me more confidence about their future, because God is in charge of it.

No matter what happens in their lives or where they go, He won't fail them or me.

"Get a Life, Neva!"
*"Here am I, and the children the Lord has given me. We
are signs and symbols in Israel from the Lord Almighty who
dwells on Mount Zion."*

- Isaiah 8:18

One recent morning found me coaching one of my teenage
daughters as she was going out the door to school. "She's old
enough. I think she can handle it, Neva. Get a life, hon," Rick
teased me good-naturedly after she left.

Choosing to ignore the tease, I went back to my morning
routine.

A half hour later found me in our schoolroom "looking for
signs of intelligent life" among our students. Square root was a
new concept to explain to my 7th grader. After that, came changing
from Celsius to Fahrenheit and vice versa with my 5th grader.
Fractions seemed to be coming pretty well for my 4th grader, but
those big division problems were still sending her for a spin. My
second grader was hearing about multiplication for the first time.

And that was just math class! Math was followed by reading,
language, penmanship, spelling, history and science. Let's face it,
home schooling isn't for wimps.

We did some other things too that day. We had lunch, did
some laundry, routine cleaning and we all enjoyed some free time.
But by the middle of the afternoon we were ready to greet our
older kids as they came home from school and sit with them and
each share about our days. Laughing at the funny things that had
happened and wiping away tears at the hurts and hard things that
we had survived.

The day ended with more chores both inside and outside,
homework and an evening meal to prepare, serve and enjoy
together.

I had thought some about Rick's tease from the morning and concluded, I don't need to get a life. I have a life. And it is full and complicated. And, you know what, it's a pretty good life. I don't care if others believe me or not. My life is wrapped up in my people, whether they are tall or short.

When I think of building my family, I'm encouraged by Nehemiah's words, "I am carrying on a great project and cannot go down."

And when I think of the sacrifice it takes to raise my family, I think of Paul's words in II Corinthians, "And I will most gladly spend and be expended for your souls. If I love you the more, am I to be loved the less?"

Our families are walls well worth building. Expenditures well worth making.

What keeps you up at night?

"Be anxious for nothing, but in everything by prayer and supplication with thanksgiving let your requests be made known to God. And the peace of God, which surpasses all comprehension, shall guard your hearts and your minds in Christ Jesus."

-Philippians 4:6,7

I could tell it was going to be a long night as I lay in the hotel room watching the numbers on the digital clock face move. "Should be about time for another number to flip. Oh, yes. Here it comes." Now it's 2:15 a.m. I had fallen asleep a couple of hours earlier, but then something had wakened me and now I could not get back to sleep.

My mind was wide awake, racing though every possible problem and dilemma that I or those I love could face.

First there was my oldest daughter. It occurred to me that,

since I was in a different time zone, she was probably driving home from her restaurant job about now. She's not the world's most experienced driver.

Then I moved on to my next daughter. A very popular baby-sitter, she had three different jobs that she was trying to make work over her school vacation. We hadn't quite figured out how to keep her three clients happy when I had left for this trip. Did she need me to help her make some decision? A quick glance at the clock showed me that it was now 2:16 a.m. Indeed, this is going to be a long night.

Then I jumped to my youngest daughter. How sad she had looked at breakfast yesterday morning. She had been crying because we were going to be gone. Was she lying in bed crying now?

2:17 a.m. For a change in pace, I began worrying about other things. Money is always an easy thing to worry about. Or health concerns of family or friends. Things I wanted to do or needed to do came next. Would I get them done? Could I get them done?

2:18 a.m. Then I switched to worrying about how bad I would look in the morning without any sleep? Would my thrashing around wake my snoring husband, sleeping beside me?

Then like a ray of sunshine the verse above popped into my mind and I began to obey it by barraging God with all kinds of prayers and requests. The simple act of throwing it upon God began to quiet my soul. My daughters are certainly all in God's quite capable hands. He'll certainly take better care of them then I could. My major "to-do" list seemed to melt under God's unchanging gaze.

And then the real miracle occurred and peaceful sleep came from knowing that God has heard all my prayers and has them all under His care.

A Lousy Grade in Science

"You slaves must obey your earthly masters in everything you do. Try to please them all the time, not just when they are watching you. Obey them willingly because of your reverent fear of the Lord. Work hard and cheerfully at whatever you do, as though you were working for the Lord rather than for people."

- Col. 3:22-23

Getting a lousy grade in science last fall might have been the best thing to ever happen to Jessica when she was a freshman. I was shocked when I picked up her grades. Attending the next parent/teacher night was my next step.

I headed to her science teacher. "Hi, I'm Mrs. Whitney," I said, as I slid into the empty seat at her table. The teacher glanced through her records and then told me that my daughter had been doing well for the first four weeks of school, but then the last two weeks, her grades had slipped – big time.

Interesting, I thought. Fall play practice had begun just a few weeks ago. I assured the teacher that my daughter would get caught up.

Needless to say, her dad and I had quite a "talk" when the three of us got together. Even our daughter was shocked that her grades could slip so much in two week's time. She was willing to do whatever it took. We told her that we wanted her to finish her commitment to the school play, but to work much harder and to use her time at school much better. She probably felt like a slave, but that was okay with us.

When Jessica got home from her last day of school last spring, she told us that she had 110% in that same science class. She had done all the extra credit that was available. She had learned to be more efficient and work a lot harder.

Even if we feel at times like we are just slaves at school or at work, that's okay. God is watching. And our service and study and hard work can be for Him. I think she learned how to work a little harder and a little more cheerfully. And God blessed her.

I'd rather be an Angel
"That night some shepherds were in the fields outside the village, guarding their flocks of sheep. Suddenly, an angel of the Lord appeared among them, and the radiance of the Lord's glory surrounded them."
                                                            - Luke 2:8,9

When my daughter Rebecca was little, she was asked to be a sheep in our church Christmas Pageant.

She didn't want to be a sheep. She wanted to be an angel. But a good friend had made this cute little sheep hat with ears hanging down and with a white sweatshirt - it made a great costume. Even if Rebecca wasn't happy, I was quite pleased.

She sat up on the stage the whole time, sobbing quietly. I finally got up and took her off the stage. I was so embarrassed. She didn't want to be a lamb; she wanted to be an angel.

You would have thought I had learned my lesson.

The next year I still had that same cute little lamb costume and so I signed Becca up to be a sheep again!

When the little kids were all lined up in the back, she started crying. One of the ushers came and got me. I had her sit with me during the Christmas program. She didn't want to be a sheep; she wanted to be an angel.

Then her last year in elementary school arrived. It was her last year to be in the church Christmas pageant and she was asked to be Mary. I was so thrilled.

She accepted the role and did a fine job with her part, but when it was all over, Becca came up to me and said, "I would rather have been an angel."

The point of this Christmas memory is that in this Christmas pageant called "Life," when God has made each of us "just a little lower than the angels," don't ever settle for anything else.

Josh's Hair

"Praise the Lord! Happy are those who fear the Lord. Yes, happy are those who delight in doing what He commands. Their children will be successful everywhere; an entire generation of godly people will be blessed."

- Psalm 112:1,2

I heard about it before I actually saw it last year. Word filtered down the Interstate from CSU. Josh, my dear, beloved, eldest son, had shaved the sides of his head and dyed the top of his hair blonde! Being the hip, happening, kind of mom that God helps me to be, I tried hard not to react too strongly when I saw it a few weeks later.

"It isn't that bad," I told myself as I got my first good look at it. "It isn't that bad. It isn't that bad."

A couple of months later when Josh returned from a summer at Myrtle Beach, South Carolina, he still had the shaved sides and the blonde hair on top, only this time it was a *lot* longer and quite unusual looking. Josh has this wiry, wavy type of hair that doesn't do well when it gets too long. Again, being the hip, happening, kind of Mom that God helps me to be, I tried hard not to say anything, although I thought it looked...

As I spent a few days with my son that month I was reminded again, that despite or in spite of his hair, it was the same old Josh that I was talking to and hanging with. A wonderful young man who really loves and respects his parents and has a heart to follow God. I decided that his hair didn't matter to me.

As a mother of seven I have been pondering on children quite a bit lately. My children, your children and just Christian children in general. I don't think that God want us to be afraid for our children and their future. We need to be faithful, work hard raising them to the best of our abilities, pray for them, and then leave them in God's loving care and protection.

Will they always act right or do right? No, of course not. Will some of them do some really dumb, stupid and even, for us, embarrassing things? Yes, probably, but we still don't need to fear for them. God has got His eye on them.

I'm reminded of Proverbs 22:15, "Foolishness is bound up in the heart of a child." When my children were younger and getting spanked regularly, I would remember that verse and try not to be dismayed when they disobeyed and needed correction. The Word says that foolishness is part of their existence. And being reminded of my most recent conversation with a highway patrolman, I know I can still be counted on for a certain measure of foolishness also.

I've thought of that verse even now as my children are older and spankings don't occur around here anymore. When my teens say or do some incredibly dumb or stupid things, I shouldn't be dismayed. They have not arrived yet!We have not arrived yet. Foolishness is still in their heart and even ours.

Braver than I wanted to be

"When you go out to fight your enemies and you face horses and chariots and an army greater than your own, do not be afraid. The LORD your God, who brought you safely out of Egypt, is with you! ...Then the officers will also say, 'Is

*anyone terrified? If you are, go home before you frighten
anyone else.' "*

- Deut. 20:1, 8

"It looks like your son has a lateral meniscus tear in his right knee. We won't know for sure until we perform the knee arthroscopy, but all signs point towards that," the knee surgeon said.

Michael's knee had locked up on a Saturday afternoon after a bruising wrestling tournament. A trip to the emergency room resulted in a set of X-rays and few concrete answers. We were told to call a surgeon Monday.

We got an appointment to see a knee specialist Monday afternoon. Surgery was set up for Wednesday. That day arrived. We took Michael in and sat and waited with him. They were running late. We waited. Finally they came. We went to the pre-op and again waited as Michael was prepped for surgery. They took him. Right before they put him under they said something about him having to be non-weight bearing for 10 weeks and possibly not fully recovered for eight or nine months.

Almost 3 ½ hours later they came out. It was over. They had had to do more major surgery than they thought, but things had gone well. There was quite a bit of damage but they felt they had repaired it.

Again we waited. Finally we were able to see him. He didn't look so good. We were able to take him home. We helped him. We ordered an ice therapy machine for his leg and set up physical therapy appointments. We picked up crutches. We iced. We elevated. We supervised simple knee exercises. We gave him his pain medication.

We tried hard not to think about what lay ahead.

I really wanted just to sit and cry many times. It had been hard to think of him undergoing anesthesia and surgery so young. Also thinking about how much Michael would have to do to recover, if he wanted to walk without limping, let alone wrestle again. Sometimes it felt overwhelming.

The verses from Deuteronomy spoke to me. They encouraged me to be braver then I felt or really wanted to be. Those verses helped me keep my emotions in check. God helped me to be tough.

How could I encourage others, if I wasn't in control myself.

Look Out, We're Being Passed!
"Thy word is a lamp unto my feet, and a light unto my path."

- Psalm 119:105

"Brace yourself, we're about to be passed!" I said to my fifteen-year-old daughter Mandy, who was just learning to drive. She was inexperienced and I was nervous, very alert, trying to guide her as much as possible.

Looking behind, I saw a vehicle approaching and did not want her to be surprised by it.

After my warning, her knuckles tightened on the steering wheel and she braced herself. Her face grimaced. She was all set.

The biked whizzed past us! We had survived.

"Try to go a little faster," I urged her. The speedometer showed 16 mph. She pressed harder on the pedal. The speedometer crept up slowly, 17, 18, 19 miles per hour.

"Mom, we're going too fast!" she exclaimed. She passed a 55 mph speed sign.

"No, we're not. You will have to drive faster if you want to drive on this road," I said firmly.

Slowly she got the car up to 35 mph and I triumphantly waved as we passed the bicyclist who had earlier passed us.

This is much like our Christian life. We think we are going full speed ahead, when really we're not. We can feel so maxed out. "Hey God, look at all I'm doing for you." When we are being passed by pedestrians or cyclists.

Focusing on the Word and obeying what we read, should be our speedometer and our guide. He will tell us how fast to drive in this Christian life and what the speed limits are. The Lord will show us just exactly how firm and how patient we should be with our children. How *fast* or how *slow* we should be with each of them.

Come Talk with Me!

"My heart has heard You say, "Come and talk with me."
And my heart responds, "LORD, I am coming."

-Psalm 27:8

I must talk with Grace today. It had been a week since we had left her in her dorm room. Although we had gotten a couple of e-mails from her, I hadn't talked to her.

I checked her schedule of classes. She should be free later this morning. I rushed through my morning tasks, including a trip to the copy center and post office. I returned home about 11 a.m.

Perfect. Grace should be back from class. She won't be heading to lunch yet.

I dialed her number. Her roommate answered. Grace was in! She came on the phone shortly.

"Hi, honey. It's Mom, I just wanted to call and talk to you," I said bravely.

I choked up. She choked up.

"I'm sorry. I didn't mean to cry," I said. "I just wanted to talk to you."

She said, "Wait. I'll get control."

I had better get control, too. She did. I did also. Then we had a nice conversation. She told me about her classes, some interesting facts about her roommate, the girls on her floor, and some of the "Rock" activities she had gone too.

I told her about my life and then said goodbye. I was glad that we had talked.

I thought about the verse I had written in my journal earlier. Just as I longed to talk with my daughter, God longs to talk to me. Just as I made an effort to connect with her, God longs to connect with me.

Our Father longs to talk with us even more than I long to talk with Grace.

Mighty Warrior

"But the LORD stands beside me like a great warrior. Before Him they will stumble. They cannot defeat me."
- Jeremiah 20:11

"We can't leave this floor out of control," my daughter thought to herself, as she and another RA answered an illegal alcohol-in-a-dorm-room incident.

They had been preparing to leave an all men's floor after writing up a roomful of college guys for drinking in their room. While they were in the "offender's" room, getting names and checking ID's, word spread to every room on the floor. And now as the girls left the hall, it seemed like all the *"men"* on that floor were now waiting in the hall.

The guys called out obscenities to Joy and her fellow RA as

they tried to walk down the crowded hallway.

"B****!" they muttered, trying to intimidate her.

Sensing God's presence and a supernatural calmness, Joy wasn't about to leave the floor until things were under control. Her whole residence hall had had a number of incidents that semester and as an RA, Joy found herself having to deal with quite a bit of "sin" and craziness.

During a recent phone conversation I had shared a verse with her. "The Lord stands beside me like a mighty warrior." Joy told me later that she pictured the Lord standing beside her in full warrior armor, as she turned to face the angry and out-of-control college boys.

"Go to your rooms now," she ordered, "or you *will* be written up!"

After they got off the floor, Joy headed to her supervisor's room and reported the incident and the vile behavior of those "men." The resident advisor was very quick to help my daughter.

I thought of that verse I had shared with her. She claimed it and hung on to it, before a mob of angry young men.

I had only claimed the verse to speak before a group of sweet Christian women. But my daughter claimed it to stand before drunken unbelievers and men at that!

It brought tears to my eyes and fear to my heart. It brought me to my knees.

Why Anthony? Why Susie?

"Put all your rebellion behind you, and get for yourselves a new heart and a new spirit. For why should you die, O people of Israel?"   - Ezekiel 18:31

Dear Anthony and Susie, (I've changed their names.)

You made me very angry this morning.

I ran into your mom. I haven't seen her for years. She was running the cash register in a grocery store. While she was ringing up another customer, I had a couple of minutes to remember your family. We worshiped together many years ago. I remember your mom's quiet voice and unusually gentle spirit.

I remember her dedication to you two.

When it was my turn, I greeted her warmly, "How nice to see you."

Your mom also gave me a warm greeting.

Then I said, "How's everything going?"

At first she looked down, then she looked up and said, "Well, Anthony and Susie aren't doing so well. They've given us lots of trouble. But they are doing better," she said determinedly, "or at least, I think Susie's coming through it."

"I'm sorry to hear that. I didn't know." I said. "I'll be praying for you and for them." I gathered my groceries and left.

Okay, Anthony and Susie, that's when I got angry. After I left, I continued thinking about your family. I thought of the pain you have caused your parents and I wondered why. Who are you trying to impress? Your parents deserve better.

No parent does everything right. We are human too. We make mistakes, but we are your parents.

I wanted to ask why. Why would kids from a good Christian home think they need to rebel? Why do you choose to shame your parents? Why do you think that you can grieve our Savior with impunity?

Are you trying to impress unbelievers? I don't think you can.

Are you trying to impress other rebellious Christian teens? Then you might be able to do so, but why would you want to? So foolish!

I am praying for you.

Sincerely, Neva

Finish Strong!
"Therefore, my beloved brethren, be steadfast, immovable, always abounding in the work of the Lord, knowing that your toil is not in vain in the Lord."

- 1 Cor.15:58

The Lord has used two words – "Finish strong!" – to encourage and inspire and gently reprove me at different times over the last few months. When I have found myself in challenging situations, those two words have been my mantra, of sorts.

In whatever you have going on in your life right now, whether it be with your children, your spouse or your ministry, finish strong. Whether you have a toddler or a teen who is keeping you up at night, finish strong. Whether you have been married two years or twenty, finish strong when different situations arise in your marriage.

Whether you are preparing to give your first Bible study or finishing up your 500th Sunday School class this Sunday, finish strong.

Getting married is easy compared to staying married over the years. Having a baby is nothing compared to raising that child. Starting a Bible study is easy; sticking it out week after week, that can be the challenge. It is easy to start something; it is oh so hard to finish. We must not lose heart in well doing.

With school, we teachers always start off the fall so well, don't we? We are so complete and so thorough with every subject. By the end of the year things can tend to come unraveled, can't they? We shouldn't let it. We should keep up the discipline that we feel right now as we begin a new term, all year long.

I have a boy who I have one more year at home with before I'll turn him over to the public school. I'm going to make this last year of home school really count. I am going to finish strong with his schooling.

On marriage, I am encouraged again by the Lord to "finish strong." I don't think I'm as young as I used to be and I certainly know that my husband isn't. In my relationship with my husband, by God's grace, I want to continue to be a supportive, loving wife, right through middle age and beyond, no matter what God throws our way.

We have all been involved in a lot of ministry over the years. Whether it is Sunday school, nursery, Bible studies, conferences, or coffees, they add up over the years. Whether you are getting started or have been at it forever, we need to keep our hearts fresh and do well in ministry.

In Luke 14 the Lord tells us to count the cost before we build a tower.

Why? Does He want us to stop, count the cost, get scared and not finish? No!

Instead He wants us to know what we are up against and how much work we have ahead. He then wants us to finish that tower and finish it strong.

Chapter 24 - Discussion Questions

1. Several of Neva's snapshots deal with trusting in God for our kids. What are specific areas that you need to trust God for - with each of your kids?

2. Sadly, worry can be a big part of parenting. What are some areas you tend to worry about with a child and what are some specific promises you need to claim?

3. Do your kids ever do anything that embarrasses you? What embarrassing areas should be dealt with? And what areas should be overlooked?

4. Often our kids do things that unnerve us or frighten us. What is our response? How do we show courage, when they show gumption?

5. After reading **Finish Strong**, what areas do you need to finish strong in?

25
Through the years:
"The Far Look"

"It is appointed unto all men to die."

- Hebrews 9:27

'The Lord's loved ones are precious to Him; it grieves Him when they die."

- Psalm 116:15

Several years ago I had the pleasure of meeting a successful graduate student whose father was a key player in the international oil business. He told me that his father had once boasted, "The world is run by 100 men, son – and I know 90 of them!"

Quite a statement. But I can do him one better.

I know the One who yanks even their chains.

He is active in our world today. He shows His love in many ways. He can even help us to die well.

Several years ago my dad died and went to be with his God. Many of you have probably already buried a parent. It is very hard. But it was such a blessing to be with him when he died.

When I first ran into the ICU, talked to the doctor, and then saw my father, I had to say, "Dad, I don't think we are gonna get out of this one." He smiled and agreed. We called all of his sons on the phone, one by one, and he smiled and wept as he listened to each of them tell him how much they loved him.

And also say good-bye.

After we hung up, I asked him if he was afraid. He got a little irritated at that point and shook his head, then looked me straight on and said, "Of course not."

"Are you eager to meet your Savior, Dad?" I asked.

He squeezed my hand pretty hard, smiled and relaxed. As a tear rolled down his cheek, he answered, "Yes, I am!" I didn't know it at the time, but those were Dad's last words. Then he fell asleep. We couldn't rouse him later and a few hours after that he passed on.

I believe God is active today. I believe He answers prayer. My prayer was that God would be gentle with my dad and help him to die well. He did this for Dad and for his whole family left behind.

I read a rather haunting quote about the time of his death. It goes like this: "Death is the sound of distant thunder at a picnic."

Thunder troubles me. We all have a gut-level reaction to the sound of thunder and it won't be denied. Death is like thunder. It gets our attention. We react to it in the deepest part of our being and it causes us to stop short amidst the crazy frenzy of our daily activity.

And that's the way it should be. Because God is active even when we see death. He is working to get our attention and to remind us of life's certain truths.

"The Lord is not slow about His promise, as some count slowness, but is patient toward you, not wishing for any to perish but for all to come to repentance."

- 2 Peter 3:9

John Wesley once said, "When I was young, I was sure of everything. After a few years, having been mistaken a thousand times, I am not half so sure."

There are days where we can sympathize with John. We are not half so sure of a great many things.

But we can be sure of this – *God is active in our world today.*

Jesus lived and walked on this rock just twenty short centuries ago. And He really did come back from the dead to reveal to all mankind that He is God. Therefore, we can know with absolute certainty that He is alive and active today. This is the logical, step-by-step truth of our faith.

We also have much anecdotal evidence to prove this truth. Obviously, if God is alive and active today, we should see evidence of His presence and activity. Granted, real life stories of God's working can sometimes be emotional and very personal – and may cause someone who doesn't believe to just chalk things up to coincidence. But since we Christians *know* He is alive, it is only natural for us to look for evidence of His presence and work.

Could I share an example that I believe reveals a Savior at work?

My grandmother was a strong believer and she led all 11 of her children to Christ – except my Uncle Ron. Over 50 years ago, she asked one of her sons (my dad) to pray for his brother Ron's salvation every day. Make that, she <u>demanded</u>

that he do it. So Dad promised. (How can you fight your mom?) Years later, she died and went to be with her God. As the years rolled by, my dad continued to pray for his brother's salvation.

Fifty years later, after living a long and hard life, Uncle Ron finally yielded to his mother's wish and gave his soul to God in the hospital. He immediately called my dad and told him that he had just become a Christian. Dad was amazed at the change in him! Ron even wanted to get out of the hospital so that he could get baptized as a believer.

Just a few weeks later, as an old man but a brand new Christian, Uncle Ron died. His children heard the gospel for the first time at his funeral, and it touched them deep in their hearts.

God answers prayer. He answered Grandma's prayer and Dad's prayer and He will answer each of our prayers for each of our family members. He may seem to be silent at times, but He is just following His own perfect timetable. We must never give up entreating God for our family's salvation.

Remember that quote from John Wesley we just read, the one about him not being "half so sure?" He went on to add, "At present, I am hardly sure of anything – except what God has revealed to me." God has revealed to John – and to us – that *He answers prayer!*

"And in the same way the Spirit also helps our weakness; for we do not know how to pray as we should, but the Spirit Himself intercedes for us with groanings too deep for words; And we know that God causes all things to work together for good to those who love God, to those who are called according to His purpose."

- Romans 8:26,28

Mike McCurry served as the press spokesman for a United States President for many years, and at times he seemed trapped and confused by the maneuverings of that administration. I'm sure that it proved more difficult than he had ever imagined. But he learned to handle his frustration with a tongue-in-cheek wit. In response to a question about the president's position on a controversial policy, Mike said, "Some of our friends are for it. Some of our friends are against it. And we're standing with our friends."

I smiled.

What can we be sure of in our lives, even if we feel pulled in two opposite directions? We can be sure of this: *God is active in our world today!* And He touches hearts.

Do you remember the title song from that Western movie "Jeremiah Johnson"? It went something like this: "The way that you wander is the way that you choose. The day that you tarry is the day that you lose." We choose where we go and how we walk through this life. We have many opportunities each day to decide how to act. God has given us this responsibility, but He has also chosen to enlarge our hearts and energize us to do the right thing. He walks with each and every one of us in our daily choices.

I may not be sure of a great many things in this life, but this I know: God walks every step of the way with me.

He is active today! My friends may stand for one thing today and my friends may stand for something else tomorrow. It makes no difference. I will stand for this: "As for me and my house, we will serve the Lord."

And for me to even be able to say this is evidence of His direct favor on my life. It is evidence that He is active today.

I will stand with my Friend, because I have a Friend who always stands with me.

"For the LORD will vindicate His people, And will have compassion on His servants; When He sees that their strength is gone."

- Deuteronomy 32:36

"Just as a father has compassion on his children, so the LORD has compassion on those who fear Him."

- Psalm 103:13

Is God active today? Yes, I believe He is. When He touches a heart, you know it.

Let me share a story that we are very proud of in our family. My little brother tells it best, so I will let him:

I was the prodigal of the family. (He wasn't the only one, but I'll let him tell his story.)

Almost fifteen years ago, I had a drug addiction to cocaine. It went on for some time and I was systematically ruining my life, my marriage and my family. But God was gracious. He got my attention and helped me to give my heart over to Him one weekend in July while I was at our cabin at the lakes.

After spending a night out on the dock praying and crying, I got up and decided to do the right thing. With the encouragement of my wife, I checked into rehab.

When I got out, I knew I needed to talk to my dad. I had shamed my family and my dad and I needed to ask his forgiveness. So I called ahead and told Dad that I would drive down and be at his house sometime Sunday afternoon. As my wife and I covered the miles toward home, I kept wondering what Dad would do when I saw him.

We pulled into the lane that led up the hill to Dad's place about sundown. He must have been waiting, looking out the window, because as I looked up the hill, I saw Dad walking down it toward the car. I kept driving up the lane as he walked down to meet us.

I stopped the car and tried to unbuckle my seat belt, open the car door and get out. But Dad pulled the door open first. I stood up and tried to mumble how sorry I was, but Dad wouldn't hear of it. He just grabbed me and hugged me and said, "You be quiet. All that matters is you're home and I love you."

I started to cry and so did Dad. Dad loved me. He accepted me. I'll never forget how he treated me at a critical time in my life.

We are all thankful for how God got our brother's attention.

We are proud of our brother and how he humbled his heart and followed his Savior.

And our whole family is also quite proud of Dad. Because of the Lord's presence in him, he acted just like the father of the prodigal son in chapter 15 of Luke.

My brother shared this story when we buried our dad a few years ago.

I am proud to have known Clay Whitney and to have been his son. All four of his other boys are equally proud. God is good and gracious and active and He can build graciousness into our hearts and into our words.

Is God active in our world today? I hope your answer is a resounding *Yes!*

Let me conclude with one more personal story.

Many years ago, a very good preacher named Crawford Loritts was invited to a weeklong, midsummer revival tent meeting held in a field near a small town in western Iowa. My hometown. God used him to touch my family. (I think he was the only black man in that whole county that week!) Here is a short piece by him about "the dash" in each of our lives.

The Dash
Have you ever been speaking when an illustration you hadn't planned came racing across your mind?

I had one of those experiences. As I was about to conclude my remarks, I said, "You know, in a few short moments we are going to take my uncle's body in this casket, roll it out and put it in the hearse in front of this church. We'll drive a few short miles to the cemetery. There will be a brief interment and shortly thereafter there will be a grave marker."

"On that grave marker will be the day of his birth. There will be a dash, and then there will be the date of his death."

I said to the people, "My uncle could not do much about the day he was born, obviously, and according to my theology, he couldn't do much about the day he died. But he did something about the dash."

"Six years ago he came to know Jesus Christ and they tell me that from then on he witnessed to everything that would come close to him."

"Birth and death are in God's hand, but you can do something about the dash."

Chapter 25 - Discussion Questions

1. Your theology will no doubt *say* that God is active in your life and in others around you. How can you test if you truly *believe* this?

2. Describe two stories, one recent and one in the distant past, where you know that God was actively working? Write these stories down for "safekeeping" so that you don't forget (read Deuteronomy 8:6-18).

3. Make a list with your spouse and your children of some events and occurrences in the last 12 months that show God's hand at work in your lives and in those close to you. Begin a personal or a family journal of these events.

26
Our Life Is Like a Coin

"The Savior is not looking for men and women who will give their spare evenings to Him – or their years of retirement. Rather, He seeks those who will give Him first place in their lives."

- William McDonald (from True Discipleship)

I would like to tell you one last story that I hope in a small way captures some of the spirit and thinking that guided us in our very first years as the Great Commission Association of Churches. Our vision – and the story of how we came to embrace it – has direct bearing on how we attempt to follow Him in our marriages and with our children. So let me get right to it.

A poet named Flora Smith wrote the following:

"I know not the way," despairing I cried.
"I am the Way," Jesus kindly replied.

"I'm searching for the truth," was my heart's
plaintive cry.
"I am the Truth," was His gentle reply.
"I'm longing for life. Oh where can it be?"
"I am the Life. Thou shalt find it in Me!"

I found Life in Him – and in Him, the Way and the Truth – many, many years ago.

My wife and I each accepted Christ as our personal Savior while we were in college. This is the *when* and the *where* of how we became Christians.

If you know Jesus Christ as your personal Savior, then you also have a starting point in your own personal spiritual journey. There is a *when* and a *where* to the beginning of your walk of faith.

And in just a little while – a relatively short time in light of eternity – we will die and be with Him. This is true for everyone who names Christ as his Redeemer. If you know and believe that He died for your sins, then you know what your future is after this mortal life. Our future will eventually be one of unbroken fellowship with the King and Guardian of our souls.

But what is God's plan for our lives in the here and now? What is God's intended future for each of us while we walk this world?

I would like to talk about this "present future" that we each possess. I do not know all of the specific details, but I do know what God's general, all-inclusive plan is for each and every born-again Christian.

It starts with the simple truth that we are owned by Another. God has redeemed us. This means that He has bought us, bought us out of this sinful world for a very clear and practical purpose. His purpose is relevant to all that we are facing in life.

I would like to spell out this purpose and talk about our shared future as believers. But to do that, I first have to go way back with my story.

In the beginning...
Thirty years ago, when our movement's pastors and church leaders were a lot younger, we all shared a common, life-changing transformation.

In the early 1970's, a number of us came to know Christ at about the same time. Many of us lived in the same town and went to the same college. In a very real way, we all experienced a brand-spanking-new spiritual awakening.

What we most clearly remember and have held onto is this – *God spoke to us! He marked our souls!*

He was very real to each of us. He not only gripped our lives with zeal for Him, but He also remade our hearts. We were "caught" in a once-in-a-lifetime way, in a way that turned our lives upside down. It was truly an awesome season in our lives.

I have no doubt that His hand was on us. As a result of His touch, we would never be the same again.

"I have found something to believe in – Jesus Christ.
I have found something to belong to – the church.
I have found something to witness for – God's
approaching kingdom."

He first sought and found us. We then found His true purpose for living, and His purpose was clear. We would drop all of our little, individual dreams and embrace His dream – and we would make life choices that reflected this shared dream.

We would stand and show our commitment and obedience to God's purpose for our lives. And we chose to stay *together* in this purpose that God had given us. We decided to embrace His gospel message as our first goal in living. Since we knew we were going to heaven, we decided that this central mission of being involved in sharing the gospel would be the central column around which we would order every decision we would ever face. We chose to do all of this *together*, as a company of men and women organized within His Church.

So as young believers some thirty odd years ago, we chose to follow Him and we chose to follow Him together.

This shared aspect to our vision was the key – and the dividing line – in our collective spiritual journey. We saw that His message of forgiveness and new life was entrusted to each of us. But we also saw that our Lord wanted us to carry out this preaching of the gospel message through "a company of men and women" united together as a church.

"Your life is like a coin. You can spend it any way you wish, but you can spend it only once."

- Miguel de Cervantes

We each decided to spend our coin (our lives) for the advancement of our Lord's kingdom on this earth and the spread of His gospel. We knew that His method to get out this gospel message was through the local church. So we pledged our lives to preach and build His kingdom *together*.

"The Savior is not looking for men and women who will give their spare evenings to Him – or their years of retirement. Rather, He seeks those who will give Him first place in their lives."

- William McDonald (from <u>True Discipleship)</u>

As we attempted to model what this *together* would look like, we never thought to look at other churches for guidance. We looked instead at just one pattern: the example of what God thought a church should look like, the pattern found in the New Testament as described in the book of Acts. There the church is put forth and defined as God intended it to be. What we read was really exciting!

This is what we saw. First, God intends for each of us to be active, impact players – workers and soldiers – in His church. Second, He designed the church to be a very straightforward, easy-to-understand, living thing.

Those first-century Christians came together as the church to accomplish a few simple, but crucial things. They first met to build up each other's faith. And so we met and purposed to build each other up through teaching, prayer, worship and the genuine sharing of our lives. We discovered that this is what genuine fellowship is all about.

We became devoted – actually we became *addicted* – to the church and how God could use each of us, working together as a team, to impact our world for Him.

What was happening was a revival of sorts. God's purpose for our lives and our shared response to it – these two things – began to grip us and proved to be a continual refreshment to our spirit. We experienced then (as we do today) an inner renewal and spiritual excitement in just being absorbed in our Master's business. This revival began to impact other people in life-changing ways. The gospel was beginning to spread!

Recently I read a quote concerning revivals that pretty much says it all: "In any awakening or revival, the first person to wake up is the Devil." So he, too, took note of what we were doing. Persecution became very real. But we did not really worry about it, because we knew in Whom we had believed, and we knew that we could entrust our lives and futures and reputations to Him. God delivered us. He is delivering us still.

About this time Jim McCotter, a fellow dad, good friend to many of us and an early leader in our movement, said something that I will never forget. It was right in the middle of a wave of very difficult persecution that we were all facing as a group of churches. Even though we were being attacked, Jim saw beyond the attack and looked ahead down the road. This is what he said:

"Join us! If you choose not to, you will still hear about us. What God is going to do through us. In good report and evil report. And you will say to yourself, 'I once knew them.'"

When you walk through battles together, God unites your hearts. The Lord used our persecutions and our shared trials to fiercely unite our hearts in a special way. Not only within each of our churches, but among our different churches and fellowships scattered across many states, and now across many nations.

"Following the Lord and doing His will, will link you heart to heart and shoulder to shoulder with the highest quality of men and women upon the face of the earth."

- Jim McCotter (early GCAC church leader)

As more leaders were raised up from within our churches, we were able to spread out to other cities. We continued our New Testament, Great Commission vision of winning the lost to Christ and then building each one up in the faith within the local churches we were planting.

Throughout our movement's history, our leaders have remained united and loyal to each other and to our shared vision regardless of geography.

God has led us each step of the way. Through Him we have done valiantly. Thousands of stories of faith and love and sacrifice could be told. Many may already have been forgotten. (We probably should have written more of them down.) But there is One who has promised that He never forgets.

George Whitefield, who is often referred to as the Billy Graham of the late 1700's, had one simple prayer. He often prayed, "God, give me a deep humility, a well-guided zeal, a burning love and a single eye – and then let men or devils do their worst."

This was our prayer, too. God has heard our prayer and in return has given our churches zeal, love and clear purpose. He has helped us to persevere and to advance His Kingdom throughout these many years.

We still hold tightly to our original vision. We believe that God wants to energize, equip and use every believer to communicate the gospel to this generation.

We believe that His vehicle to accomplish this is the local church. The church is a living, growing thing. We believe that the church, His church, is sufficient to accomplish the task of reaching the world. And we believe that the church that embraces God's New Testament pattern will remain God's primary vehicle by which He will speak the gospel to this world.

So we invite every person, every man and woman, every believer to commit his and her heart afresh to this purpose and vision.

This is where we are going. It is not just our history – it is also our future!

Often as believers we are so caught up in our everyday lives that we forget where and how He has led us. We forget how, in the words of the old hymn, He has "brought us safe thus far." If we have forgotten who we are and what He has done for us, then we may also forget where we are going. We can almost lose our perspective.

That is one reason why I am writing this history of our heart. My desire is to help us stay focused in this battle, to help us finish strong.

Until we run out of time on this earth, we will remain steady in our resolve to win souls to Christ and to do this through our local fellowships. We will remain united in this shared cause. We will not doubt the vision, even if it takes longer than we initially expected.

In Habakkuk, chapter 2, the Lord writes,

> *"Record the vision.*
> *And inscribe it on tablets,*
> *That the one who reads it may run.*
> *For the vision is yet for the appointed time;*
> *It hastens toward the goal, and it will not fail.*
> Though it tarries, wait for it;
> *For it will certainly come…"*

In the New Living Translation, it goes like this:

> *"Then the LORD said to me, "Write my answer in large, clear letters on a tablet, so that a runner can read it and tell everyone else. But these things I plan won't happen right away. Slowly, steadily, surely, the time approaches when the vision will be fulfilled. If it seems slow, wait patiently, for it will surely take place. It will not be delayed."*

God is doing a great work. Slowly, steadily, surely, He is accomplishing this vision. He started this association of churches in a simple, precious way: by writing this vision on the tablets of men's hearts. I know this to be true, for I was there.

He wrote this vision in each pastor's heart and in the hearts of many other heroic men and women in our churches. I know this to be true, for I was there when He did it.

It remains true today.

Your leaders have never ceased to believe in this vision. In good times and in bad times. In good report or evil report. Through great blessings and great trials. Wherever we are scattered on the face of the globe.

You are involved in the great work of building His church.

Our Lord Himself has led us – together – from glory to glory. Don't ever forget it.

If you are a long-time laborer in His fields, press on! Be stouthearted! Do not faint or grow weary in well doing, for in due time you shall reap.

If you are a seeker, if you want great purpose for your life, join us!

"Following the Lord and doing His will, will link you heart to heart and shoulder to shoulder with the highest quality of men and women upon the face of the earth."

I would challenge you afresh, join us! Don't miss your chance to spend your life in a noble cause. You won't regret it. Remember, your life is like a coin. But you can spend it only once.

Keep pressing,
Rick

Chapter 26 – Discussion Questions

1. How committed are you to living out this vision <u>together</u> with others in your church?

2. How devoted are you to these people? How can you measure this devotion?

3. How will you keep this vision burning hot in your heart? Or, to look at it another way, what "extinguishes" this vision in your heart, and what will you do about it?

Appendix

Parenting Workshop, first handout

1. Parenting problems can be _____,
    but the answers are fundamentally _____.

2. Every family is unique, however we can still _____
    parenting _____.

3. Our children are more _____ than they are
    _____.

4. Our children are naturally _____ and will never
    _____ outgrow it.

5. Our children need more than our love and attention. They
    need _____ to succeed in life.

6. Our children are on a journey, moving from _____
    responsibility to _____ responsibility.

7. The greatest need for being successful parents is to have
    strong _____ and strong _____.

Parenting Workshop, second handout

1 Kings 1:6

New American Standard
And his father had never _____ him at any time by asking, "Why have you done so?" And he was also a very handsome man; and he was born after Absalom.

King James Version
And his father had not _____ him at any time in saying, "Why hast thou done so?"

New International Version
And his father had never ` _____ with him by asking, "Why do you behave as you do?"

Berkeley Version
His father had never _____ him by asking, "Why do you do so and so?"

The Living Bible
Now his father, King David, had never _____ him at any time – not so much as by a single scolding.

Parenting Workship, third handout

"Train up a child in the way he should go,
Even when he is old he will not depart from it. "

- Proverbs 22:6

1. First then, if you will train your children rightly, train them in
   the way they should go, and not in the way that they _____.

2. Train your children with an abiding persuasion on your mind
   that _____ depends upon you.

3. Train them to a habit of _____.

4. Train them to a _____ of always redeeming
   the time.

5. Train them with a constant fear of _____ -indulgence.

6. Train them remembering continually how God trains His
   children.
   - He _____.
   - He _____.
   - He _____.

7. Train them with tenderness, _____ _____ and
   patience, continually reminding them of the promises of God,
   the power of prayer and the value of our faith.

- from <u>The Duties of Parents</u> by J.C. Ryle, 1888

Parenting Workshop, fourth handout

Seven Days of Prayer for Our Family

(The ABC's)

Sunday   1. We would be _____
                   by God's work in our family.

Monday   2. Our children would do _____
                   works than their parents.

Tuesday   3. The kids would have _____
                   values and character.

Wednesday   4. All my _____ would be saved.

Thursday   5. The children would become _____
                   spouses and find good mates.

Friday   6. Our family would be _____
                   from moral impurity.

Saturday   7. That we'd be a _____
                   commission family.

Parenting Workshop, fifth handout

Seven Practical Goals for My Children

(The Building Blocks)

1. That they would have a _____ of God.

2. That they would _____ and _____ the Bible.

3. That they would _____ the Bible's stories.

4. That they would be individuals who _____.

5. That they would value _____, to God and others.

6. That they would be _____ and _____.

7. That they would be _____ and eager to _____.

"What we have a right to expect of any boy is that he shall turn out to be a good man. The chances are strong that he will not be much of a man unless he is a good deal of a boy.

He must not be a coward, a weakling, a bully, a shirk, nor a prig. He must work hard and play hard. He must be clean-minded and clean-lived and able to hold his own under all circumstances and against all comers.

It is only on these conditions that he will turn out to be the kind of man of whom we may really be proud.

In life, as in a football game, the principle to follow is – 'Hit the line hard, do not foul, and do not shirk; but hit the line hard!'

- Teddy Roosevelt

Parenting Workshop, sixth handout

The measure of a boy/girl

>   *"Train up a child in the way he _____ go."* Pv. 22:6

1. Obedient
    >   *"Children, be obedient to your parents in _____*
    >   *things."* Col. 3:20

2. Pays attention
    >   *"My son, give attention to my _____."* Pv. 4:20

3. Learns to share, is considerate of others
    >   *"The _____ boy will be rich."* Pv. 11:25

4. Accepts discipline without anger or pouting
    >   *"A child who gets his _____ way brings shame*
    >   *to his mother."* Pv. 29:15

5. Responds to direction to control emotions
    >   *"A wise son _____ his father's discipline."* Pv. 13:1

6. Starts building a reputation
    >   *"It is by his deeds that a lad _____*
    >   *himself."* Pv. 20:11

7. Starts developing good work habits
    >   *"In all labor there is profit, but mere _____ leads*
    >   *only to poverty."* Pv. 14:23

8. Can handle pain
    >   *"The _____ of a boy can endure his pain."* Pv. 18:14

Parenting Workshop, seventh handout

The measure of a teen

   "Give me your _____, my son." Pv. 23:26

1. Has a sense of purpose
   "Let your eyes look _____ ahead." Pv. 4:25

2. Has good work habits (Is a self-starter)
   "He who _____ in harvest is a son who acts shamefully." Pv. 10:5

3. Distinguishes himself by good deeds
   "It is by his _____ that a lad distinguishes himself." Pv. 20:11

4. Is strong against peer pressure
   "My son, if sinners entice you, do not ____." Pv. 1:10

5. Develops the right friends
   "He who ____ with wise men will be wise." Pv. 13:20

6. Is not naive
   "The naive _____ everything." Pv. 14:15

7. Values parent's instruction in his heart
   "My son, do not _____ the teaching of your mother." Pv. 6:20

8. Trusts in God's Word
   "Trust in the Lord with _____ your heart." Pv. 3:5

9. Manages his emotions
    "He who has a _____ *spirit is a man of understanding."* Pv. 17:27

10. Has good speech
    "My inmost being will rejoice when your lips speak what is _____*."* Pv. 23:16

11. Not foolish, is sensible
    "A wise son makes a father _____*."* Pv. 15:20

12. Has a good countenance
    "A joyful heart makes a _____ *face."* Pv. 15:13

13. Respects others, protects siblings
    "A _____ *is born for adversity."* Pv. 17:17

14. Honors all women, specifically his _____.
    Pv. 10:1, 15:20, 20:20, 23:22, 23:25, 29:15, 30:11

15. Knows how to handle suffering
    "My son, do not _____ *the discipline of the Lord."* Pv. 3:11

16. Is trustworthy and faithful
    "A faithful man will _____ *with blessings."* Pv. 28:20

17. Has biblical understanding of grace and forgiveness
    "How blessed is the man who ____ *always."* Pv. 28:14

The greatest need for successful parents is to have strong _____ and strong _____.

Dating? Romance? God's Will?

The subject of this paper is whether Christians should be involved in dating.

The Bible does not specifically instruct us as to the best way to find a wife, nor does it deal with the subject of romantic relationships outside of marriage. In the absence of clear instruction or commands either promoting or forbidding a specific action, we must develop our thinking based on biblical principles that relate to this topic. Our culture has already established a cultural norm for dating.

My question is, "Can our culture's system of dating be supported by biblical principles?"

It is very important that we first define our terms. For the purposes of this paper, I will define dating (or recreational dating) as *"the practice of developing a one-on-one romantic relationship, without the intent or commitment of marriage."*

This definition, I believe, represents the attitude and actions of many.

This is not the same as spending time with the specific purpose of determining whether the Lord might be leading in marriage.

Several passages to consider as you work through a number of questions that always arise in our minds are:

"But put on the Lord Jesus Christ, and make no provision for the flesh in regard to its lusts."

- Rom 13:14

"Do not sharply rebuke an older man, but rather appeal to him as a father, to the younger men as brothers, the older women as mothers, and the younger women as sisters, in all purity."

- 1 Tim 5:1,2

"And this I say for your own benefit; not to put a restraint upon you, but to promote what is seemly, and to secure undistracted devotion to the Lord."

- 1 Cor 7:35

Here are the questions:

What are the goals of recreational dating? One goal that could be considered positive is learning to relate to members of the opposite sex. A consideration to be made when promoting this goal is whether it will be helpful in any relationship after marriage, except with our spouse? Does practicing this romantic, intimate kind of relationship truly enable us to relate better with members of the opposite sex? It would be very questionable. The actions learned will not relate to any other opposite sex relationship we have during our lifetime.

We were made by God to have only one, intimate, romantic relationship and that would be with our spouse. Considering the difficulty that many men and women find in relating on a brother/sister level, would it be better to practice our friendships in a non-romantic way, rather than the emotional and relational "Pandora's box" of romantic involvement?

There are also many goals associated with dating that would not be considered positive. These goals would be hard to justify biblically. Here are a few of them:

- *"I have mine"* - The tension and pressure that many young people (especially women) feel, to have a personal relationship that fulfills their felt need to feel loved and special.

- *"Acting like an adult"* - There is great pressure to look and act like a grown-up. To be adult like, there is strong pressure to have a meaningful, personal, romantic relationship. This dating enters into almost a "pseudo-marriage."

• *"I am attractive or desirable"* - This hits both sexes equally, but each have different motives. Young men, I believe, struggle in the area of proving their masculinity (as our fallen society defines this) by proving they can "get as many girls as they possibly can." Maybe this is an over-simplification, but these are real pressures our world hits us with.

We each must also consider the fruit of our world's way of dating. What happens when we end a casual, dating relationship? Rarely if ever are two people, whether believers or not, who become involved in a romantic relationship and then "break up", ever as close or friendly after the break-up as before they crossed this line into romantic involvement. What is it that causes this tension? Is it necessary? Is it desirable?

Trying out a potential mate does not necessarily prove either compatibility or success in a relationship. The divorce rate is higher for those who cohabit prior to marriage than for those who do not – not to mention that it is immoral and offends our Savior. Could it be that the necessary ingredient for a successful marriage is commitment, and not compatibility or physical attraction?

Does a string of involvements and break-ups help us or harm us in our ability to commit? Is a romantic investment in a person who is not your spouse – or who is not going to be your spouse – a worthwhile endeavor? Is recreational dating (romantic involvement) an acceptable expression of agape love for the Christian man and woman? Does recreational dating promote or hinder purity, godliness and selflessness?

There is one biblically sanctioned distraction to our devotion to the Lord – marriage! Does recreational dating qualify as an acceptable distraction? What do you think?

I join with Paul in saying that it is not my goal to put restraints on or to limit anyone's fun. My goal is to help every man and woman ensure that their fun is pure and honoring to God. It is my hope that young women will be spared the emotional agony of giving away their heart and then having it broken. I also hope that young men will be spared our society's distorted view of women as either a conquest or plaything, but rather to learn to love a girl as the protector that God has called him to be. I hope that each one will be spared the guilt, pain and anxiety of going farther than they intended.

My prayer is that Christians would consider the benefits of avoiding romantic involvement until they are ready to commit to the contract of marriage. In marriage our Lord wants us to be passionate. He designed us this way. But His designed outlet for our passion is through marriage. He does not want us to get all "steamed up" and not be married. He is not a cruel God. That is why He tells us to wait for marriage.

My prayer is that young men and women might then present themselves to their spouse – morally, physically and emotionally pure. What a great wedding gift that would be to give each other and how honoring this is to our Savior!

- Pat Sokoll, Solon, Iowa

If you still are having trouble corralling your son or daughter, then the following form might possibly be of help.

APPLICATION FOR PERMISSION TO DATE MY DAUGHTER

NOTE: This application will be incomplete and rejected unless accompanied by a complete financial statement, parole officer's report, job history, lineage and current medical report from your doctor.

NAME_____

DATE OF BIRTH_____

HEIGHT_____ WEIGHT____ BOY SCOUT RANK _____

SOCIAL SECURITY#_____I.Q. _____

DRIVER'S LICENSE #_____ G.P.A._____

HOME ADDRESS_____

CITY/STATE_____ZIP_____

Do you have one MALE and one FEMALE parent?_____

Number of years parents married: _____

Do you own a van?_____A truck with oversized tires?_____

A waterbed?_____

In 50 words or less, what does "LATE" mean to you?

In 50 words or less, what does "DON'T TOUCH MY DAUGHTER" mean to you?

In 50 words or less, what does "ABSTINENCE" mean to you?

Church you attend?_____ How often?_____
When would be the best time to interview your father?_____
Your mother?_____ Your pastor? _____
What do you want to be if you grow up? _____

Answer by filling in the blank. Please answer freely; all answers are confidential.

A. If I were shot, the last place on my body I would want to be wounded is _____.

B. If I were beaten, the last bone I would want broken is

_____.

C. A woman's place is in the _____.

D. The one thing I hope this application does not ask me about is

_____.

E. When I first meet a girl, the thing I notice about her is

_____.

I SWEAR THAT ALL INFORMATION SUPPLIED ABOVE IS TRUE AND CORRECT TO THE BEST OF MY KNOWLEDGE UNDER PENALTY OF DEATH.

_____

Signature (that means sign your name)

(Thank you for your interest. Please allow four to six years for processing. You will be contacted in writing if you are approved. Please do not try to call or write.)

summitview - Loveland

"Salt Students" - Purpose, Plan and Standards

Our Purpose

Our student ministry exists to be "salt and light" in this world. To reach other students (nonbelievers and believers) and connect them to God through our own relationship with God and our parents.

Our Plan/Our Method

These five parts to our plan deal with *"all the bases."* If we pay attention to all five of these areas, we will accomplish our shared purpose - as a team of committed, young Christians - to reach out to our world with the gospel.

1. Regular, father-led, weekly Bible study, prayer, and fellowship.
2. Organized and *unorganized* Outreach in our High Schools and with our friends.
3. Conferences, get-aways, over-nighters; where our hearts can be deeply challenged.
4. Mucho, mucho service and work. Not just sitting around and hoping someone entertains us, but rolling up our sleeves!
5. Leadership development of our upper-classmen.

Our Standards/*"Honoring One Another"*

As we meet together and work our plan, the following standards will allow us to accomplish our purpose as a group of Christian teens and allow us to fulfill His will in our lives.

1. We will be careful in our physical affection. No groping, or hanging on, members of the opposite sex, no prolonged *"brotherly love"* hugs, no smooching or sitting on each other's laps, no backrubs, etc.
2. No being alone in guy/girl situations. Either on walks or in cars, etc. We will get to know each other all together.
3. No swearing, or crude language or coarse talk, jokes, etc.
4. There is a dress code! No see-through shirts, underwear revealed, jeans that reveal underwear, suggestive clothing, etc.
5. No smoking, tobacco, obviously no drugs or alcohol, etc.
6. **Honor one another above yourself !**

Prairie View Community Church

Here is a "Plan of Action" for our Teens at **Prairie View**. It reflects what we have been doing for several years.

It has Five elements —

1. Weekly Bible Study.

A. Dads will carry the bulk of the teaching. Reflecting on the enclosed Daylights, we would suggest that several fathers of teens be called upon to teach at times. These Dads could teach an individual night's study or a short series. It seems important to allow many fathers to be involved in the spiritual instruction of their sons or daughters.

Dads need to be teaching, instructing and guiding. And it would be good for our youth to be listening to their fathers in this context. We need to be leading them, spiritually. Just as some of us have taught Sunday School, I think that Dads need to also have an opportunity, *if they want it*, to be involved with their teens in this way.

B. Every Tuesday night, we would also encourage not only group prayer with all of the teens and discussion of that night's lesson, but also a brief testimony from a teen. Tuesday night could be a great place for every teen to have a chance to share how they came to know Christ. Just one testimony a night. Five minutes long, at the most.

It would be good practice for all of our youth. Every young man and woman needs to know how to share their testimony in a straight-forward way, stay on track and to be able to speak before their peers.

2. Organized and *Unorganized* Outreach.

We hope for at least three activities during every calendar school year. Activities designed as a place where our teens can bring their friends to a party or event and at that party there would be good food, good fellowship **and the gospel would be shared!** We have had Snow-tubing, Cook-outs, Costume parties, Christmas parties, etc.

Here are three target outreach activities:
   a.) a October Saturday Night Cook-out.
   b.) a Christmas Saturday Night Party.
   c.) a March Saturday Night Party. *(this party is held about a month before our Spring Teen Conference, a conference that is designed for us to be able to bring a lost friend to.)*

Our teens must be involved in sharing their faith! We need to provide places and events where they can bring their friends and speak up for their Lord, together. Our teens cannot have a "Christian ghetto" mentality where they just hide out with their Christian friends. I would stress these three outreach activities and to **do them well**!

3. Conferences.

Getting away for conferences are critical in shaping the spirit of our youth. Extended times away can really leave lasting spirit and soul impressions.

With this in mind I would propose the following:

a.) a **Friday Night Lock-In**. Early in the school year (late

August / early September) it could be very strategic to have a Friday Night Prayer Meeting for the fall term. We would just do it locally for the Prairie View youth. We could provide supper that night and then prayer and sharing and encouragement. There would be some teaching, singing, worship, etc, but mainly a lot of prayer. It could go till Midnight and then the boys and men would head to another house to sleep and the girls would stay where they are. Then meet again for Breakfast and a brief time of prayer and wrap up and sharing the following morning.

It would be cheap, local, easy to organize, and focused on prayer in light of the school year - dead ahead..

This is _not_ an Out-reach conference.

b.) **Front Range Spring Teen Conference.** This conference is for our churches youth, here along the Front Range and it is designed for our teens to be able to bring their lost friends to it. It is somewhat local, still not too expensive and God has used it for many years to see a number of our son's and daughter's friends saved. Friends they have made during the school year. We do it in the spring so that they can have almost a full school year to build their friendships and be able to bring their lost friends with them.

This _is_ an Out-reach conference.

c.) **High School Leadership Training (HSLT).** This conference is almost a week long, and is designed for the serious High School Christian. At this conference there is a lot of teaching and a lot of opportunity for our youth to be involved in sharing their faith. It costs over $200 and represents a pretty significant commitment from each of our youth, especially when they go out sharing their faith. (cold turkey)

This conference is designed for the committed high school Christian.

4. Service.

A hallmark of our church's youth has been their willingness to jump in, roll up their sleeves and work. Without our teens and their service, we probably would not have a church. We do not want to lose this aspect of a teen's spiritual growth. Just as we have had many opportunities to serve over the years – we need to give our teens opportunity to genuinely roll up their sleeves in the service of the church. In fact we want to increase it all the more. I don't think it pleases the Lord, nor builds our youth, to treat them like *"prima-donna's."*

"The thing that impresses me most about America, is the way parents obey their children."

\- Duke of Windsor

"The best security I can give my children is an unquenchable thirst for hard work."

\- Anonymous

Our teens need to continue to serve in our church. Sunday morning set-up, tear-down, setting up chairs, showing hospitality to our church's visitors *(especially those teens that walk in the door with their parents),* helping out with Nursery, Promise Land, performing musically with the worship team, etc. God will bless them.

Because of their service and good work habits and their lack of any kind of *"cliqueishness," we really don't think our youth take a back seat to anyone. They are exemplary.*

"Not so with you. Instead, whoever wants to become great among you must be your servant, and whoever wants to be first must be your slave—just as the Son of Man did not come to be served, but to serve, and to give His life as a ransom for many."

- Matthew 20:26-28

"Neither intelligence nor talent is as valuable as the knack for hard work. Give your child this knack."

- Anonymous

5. Leadership Development.

Every year we always need to be re-grouping and looking to our upper classmen to set the pace. Our Juniors and Seniors need this opportunity. Just as previous high school graduates have been very involved in serving, coordinating and leading, so too, we need to ask the next group to *"step-up to the plate."* They need to be brought into teen ministry planning and they need to "own" their plans.

But they also need to be guided. Often there is a lot of energy and ideas, but very little follow through with teens. They are often taught to brainstorm in high school, but they don't always get a lot done. They might get excited and want to do a lot, but very little gets accomplished without our guidance. So we dads will work together with them.

We need to bring upper classmen together, present this overview, and have them fill-in-the-blanks.

But I think a Plan like this with these five different elements, is important to give them as a model. Otherwise their own plan, (on a blank sheet), could easily forget one of these five important functions.

Summary

Just to review—fathers, we can't assume that our teens will turn out without our serious involvement. These five points deal with *"all the bases."*

1.   Regular Bible study and fellowship.
2.   Outreach in their own world and field—their high school.
3.   Conferences, get-away's, where their heart can be deeply challenged.
4.   Mucho, mucho service and work. Not just sitting around and hoping someone entertains them.
5.   Leadership development of our upper-classmen.

Here are two Daylights, that capture this example of a father led, church based, teen ministry model.

Who has his Heart?

"My son, give me your heart and let your eyes keep to my ways..."

- Proverbs 23:26

"Our mouth has spoken freely to you, O Corinthians, our heart is opened wide. You are not restrained by us, but you are restrained in your own affections. Now in a like exchange—I speak as to children—open wide to us also."

- 2 Cor. 6:11-13

Have you ever asked yourself the question, *"Do I really have the heart of my daughter? Do I really have the heart of my son?"* I like the clarity of this Proverb, where the father simply asks, "Give me your heart." But what if we don't have their heart? Is there anything we can say or do, to warm up a relationship that for all outward appearances, might be drifting away?

I think so. The key is revealed in Paul's example, shown towards those believers in Corinth. Before Paul asks for their heart—he reminds them that he has already given his heart away. And they knew it.

The following is a good example of a young man who appreciates his dad. His father, a deacon in our church and a good man, has caught his son's heart. Notice how Dad first did it;

"As long as I can remember, my dad played basketball and encouraged me as well. My first toy was a little basketball that squeaked, and I received my first hoop for my third Christmas. Even at that age, my dad never just let me win. In fact, I was never able to beat him until high school. Because of this, I will never forget the moment I won. It was on a running jump shot down the left side; it wasn't pretty, but it went in.

My dad has also greatly encouraged my interest in computers. When I was little, we would literally spend hours playing computer games together. Later he taught me how to install software, which let me serve my school. When I was in eighth grade, he started his own computer business, where I have worked alongside him, ever since."

But this Dad didn't stop with the basketball and computers. He took another critical step and got involved in the spiritual instruction of his son. Tune in tomorrow.

Who has his Heart? – part 2

"In place of your fathers will be your sons; You shall make them princes in all the earth."

- Psalms 45:16

Yesterday I let a young man, in his own words, share how much he appreciates his Dad. Dad did a few things to capture the boy's heart. Today I want to let him share probably the most critical thing this Dad did. What was it? He got involved in the spiritual instruction of his son. He didn't delegate this. He rolled up his sleeves and jumped right in.

But I will let the boy write in his own words just what dear old Dad did.

"When I was a freshman, my dad helped start a teen Bible study for my friends. It began with only five people, but now as many as thirty come on a weekly basis. The Bible study has gotten me more involved in church and helped me develop many lasting friendships. My dad has always been a great role model for me; but now that I am one of the oldest in the group, I have the opportunity to lead and be a role model for the younger kids. I know my life would be different if my dad had not started the Bible study.

Writing this essay, I was, for the first time, disappointed with a length restriction. Five hundred words are not nearly enough to describe the impact my dad has made on my life. But until this essay, I had never really thought much about it. I have the same interests, looks, voice, personality, and even the same sense of humor as my dad. Some might say I'm "a chip off the old block," but that's fine with me.

Mark Twain once declared, "It is a wise child that knows

its own father, and an unusual one that unreservedly approves of him." What kind of teenager considers an expression like "Chip off the old block" a compliment? I do. Because of my great admiration for my dad, he has had, and still does have, an incredible influence on almost every facet of my life."

Sincerely, Jon Martin

And I guess that's all I have to say about that.